# COMPUTERS IN YOUR LIFE

*By the Author*

THE NEW EARTH BOOK

THE NEW WATER BOOK

THE NEW AIR BOOK

THE NEW FOOD BOOK
*with Gilda Berger*

# COMPUTERS IN YOUR LIFE

MELVIN BERGER

Thomas Y. Crowell New York

Computers in Your Life

For information address Thomas Y. Crowell Junior Books, 10 East 53rd Street, New York, N. Y. 10022. Published simultaneously in Canada by Fitzhenry & Whiteside Limited, Toronto.

---

*Library of Congress Cataloging in Publication Data*
Berger, Melvin.
Computers in your life.
SUMMARY: Explains how computers work and discusses their increasing importance in more and more areas of day-to-day life.
1. Computers—Juvenile literature. 2. Electronic data processing—Juvenile literature. [1. Computers. 2. Electronic data processing] I. Title.
QA76.23.B47 001.64 80-2452
ISBN 0-690-04100-4
ISBN 0-690-04101-2 (lib. bdg.)

---

1 2 3 4 5 6 7 8 9 10
First Edition

## *Acknowledgements*

*Many individuals, corporations, schools and colleges, and government agencies helped me in the writing of this book. I thank them all. I would like, however, to express my special gratitude to: AT & T (Fran Makula), Apple Computer, Inc. (Lynn Wedel), Milton Bradley Company (George E. Chartier), Bureau of the Census, Department of Commerce (Dan Bailey and Henry H. Smith), Computalker Consultants (Lloyd Rice), Computer Curriculum Corp. (Mark Ogborn), Criminal Justice Services, State of New York (Adam F. D'Alessandro), Datatrol, Inc. (Frederick Balas), Department of the Air Force (Lt. Col. Richard L. Fuller), EDP Security, Inc. (Robert P. Santis), Evans and Sutherland (Ted Naanes), Fidelity Electronics, Ltd. (Peter Nasca), Ford Motor Company (Charles G. Olbricht), Great Neck Library (Joseph Covino), Honeywell Information Systems, Inc. (Faye Kittredge), IBM (Richard E. Coyle), Koala 'T' Toys, Inc. (Gerald W. Spilman), McDonnell Douglas Corp. (John Bickers), Motorola, Inc. (Carole Book), NASA (Les Gaver), Nassau County Medical Center (Michael M. DeLuca), National Institutes of Health (Jerry Gordon), National Maritime Research Center (Joseph Pugliese, Jerry Reardon, Harry Rossman, Albert Stwertka, Stanley Wheatley), Dr. Monroe Newborn, New York City Police Department (Deputy Inspector Peter J. Prezioso, Lt. James Mooney, Police Officer John E. Haas), Secretary of Defense, Selchow and Righter (Edward J. Rivoir), Stanford University (Patrick Suppes), Telesensory Systems, Inc. (Jan Boomsliter), Texas Instruments, Inc. (R. M. Perdue, Richard Wiggins), Unimation, Inc. (Ellen D. Mohr), United Airlines (Eileen Golab).*

*Picture credits: ATT, pages 7, 14, 32, 33; Apple Computer, Inc., 89; Computer Curriculum Corporation, 71; Datatrol, Inc., Hudson, Mass., 65; Fidelity Electronics Ltd., Miami, Fla. 88; Ford Motor Company, 42, 43; Great Neck Library, N.Y., 39; Honeywell Information Systems, 68; IBM, 10, 13, 17, 20 (top and bottom), 59, 99; Japan Trade Center, 47; Milton Bradley Company, 82, © 1978 by the Milton Bradley Company; National Maritime Research Center, Kings Point, N.Y., 54, 55; Dr. M. Newborn, 86; SPRING 3100, New York City Police Department, 93; Playskool, Inc., 83, © 1978 by Playskool, Inc.; Beverly L. Shea, Danwille School District, Ill., 76, photograph by Rick Nelson; Telesensory Systems, Inc., 73 (top and bottom); Unimation, Inc., Danbury, Conn., 67; United Airlines, 49; U.S. Air Force, 15, 109; Bureau of the Census, U.S. Department of Commerce, 4, 12, 103 (top and bottom), 104.*

# CONTENTS

# 1 COMPUTERS IN ACTION

The mother rushes her three-year-old son to the hospital's emergency room.

"My baby has a very high fever," she explains. "He is shaking all over."

The doctor examines the boy right away. He draws a sample of blood from the boy's arm, and rushes it over to the laboratory. The lab worker places it in a large machine with a built-in computer.

In less than a minute the machine tests the blood and prints out the results. The doctor reads the findings. They tell him what is wrong with the child. He gives the youngster an injection. Half an hour later, the boy is playing and smiling.

To the police officers in the patrol car, it looks like a typical case of a car passing a red light. They put on their flashing lights, and speed up to catch the car. But the other driver begins going even faster.

"This might mean trouble," says one of the officers. "Check the license on the computer. See what you get."

His partner types the car's license number on the tiny computer mounted on the dashboard of the police car. Green letters start to spell out words on the small screen. "Stolen car. Used in armed robbery. Dangerous. Proceed with caution."

The police car pulls ahead. It forces the other car to stop. The two officers come out with drawn pistols. They arrest the driver, and bring him to the police station for questioning.

Four times a year, all the classes at Kennedy High School were dismissed at noon. The teachers spent those afternoons entering grades on the students' report cards.

Now there is no early dismissal at the end of each marking period. The teachers mark the students by filling in little boxes on computer cards. The computer then automatically reads each card, and prints out report cards for the entire student body.

Carla and three of her friends decide to go to a New York Jets football game one Sunday afternoon. But no one has any money. All the banks are closed.

Carla, though, has a special bank card. She goes to the closed bank office. Placing her card in a slot on the outside of the bank, she types in various numbers on the keyboard below.

The keyboard sends a message to the bank's computer. The computer automatically takes the money from her account. It pushes out the bills through another opening in the wall.

Computers help to save lives and catch criminals. They are used to fill out report cards and transact bank business after hours. In hospitals and in police work, in schools and banks, in homes and airports, in factories and stores, in outer space and on the highways, in laboratories and on farms—computers are changing the way we live. In fact, no matter what you do, or where you do it, you can be sure that there is a computer in your life!

# 2 WHAT IS A COMPUTER?

## A PROBLEM SOLVER

A computer is a human tool. Like other tools, it helps people work better. A computer can perform a number of operations at very high speeds. It can add, subtract, multiply, and divide. It can compare numbers, and decide which is bigger and which is smaller. It can arrange and organize long lists of separate items in any order. It can store any number of facts. And it can communicate with its human users.

The computer was invented long, long ago. The inventor's name is unknown, but whoever it was, he or she was the first person to use fingers as a counting machine.

Over the following centuries, many mechanical counting machines were invented. They all had moving parts. The ancient Chinese abacus, for example, has moving beads on a frame. Herman Hollerith's 1890 tabulating machine has metal rods that punch holes in cards.

A 1890 tabulating machine.

## FIRST GENERATION COMPUTERS

The modern age of computers began in 1946. That was when the first electronic computer was built. It did not have any moving parts. Calculations were done by controlling the flow of electricity. It was a giant step forward compared to all of the mechanical devices used before.

This computer, called ENIAC (Electronic Numerical Integrator and Computer) was huge. It weighed thirty tons and covered fifteen hundred square feet. The flow of electrons was controlled by vacuum tubes. The tubes looked like twenty thousand glowing light bulbs.

All of the computers built in the 1950s relied on vacuum tubes. The tubes took up a lot of space, used a lot of electricity, produced a lot of heat, and were not very reliable. That is why, in 1959, engineers welcomed the invention of small, solid electronic devices called transistors. Transistors could be used instead of the vacuum tubes.

## SECOND AND THIRD GENERATION COMPUTERS

When transistors replaced the vacuum tubes in computers, they lowered the price of computers about 85 percent. What's more, they ran a thousand times faster. Computers became cheaper, faster, smaller, and more reliable. Transistor-based computers, built during the 1960s, were called second generation machines.

The third generation of computers arrived in the mid-1970s. Miniature integrated circuits were introduced around that time. They are called miniature because the electronic parts are tiny or microscopic in size. They are called integrated because all of these parts are built onto a single chip no larger than your fingernail, made of the mineral silicon. Silicon is a very abundant chemical element found in sand. And they are called circuits because the flow of electrons through these devices performs all the work of the computer. These third generation computers are one-tenth the size of second generation computers. They are also about one hundred times faster and one thousand times cheaper to run.

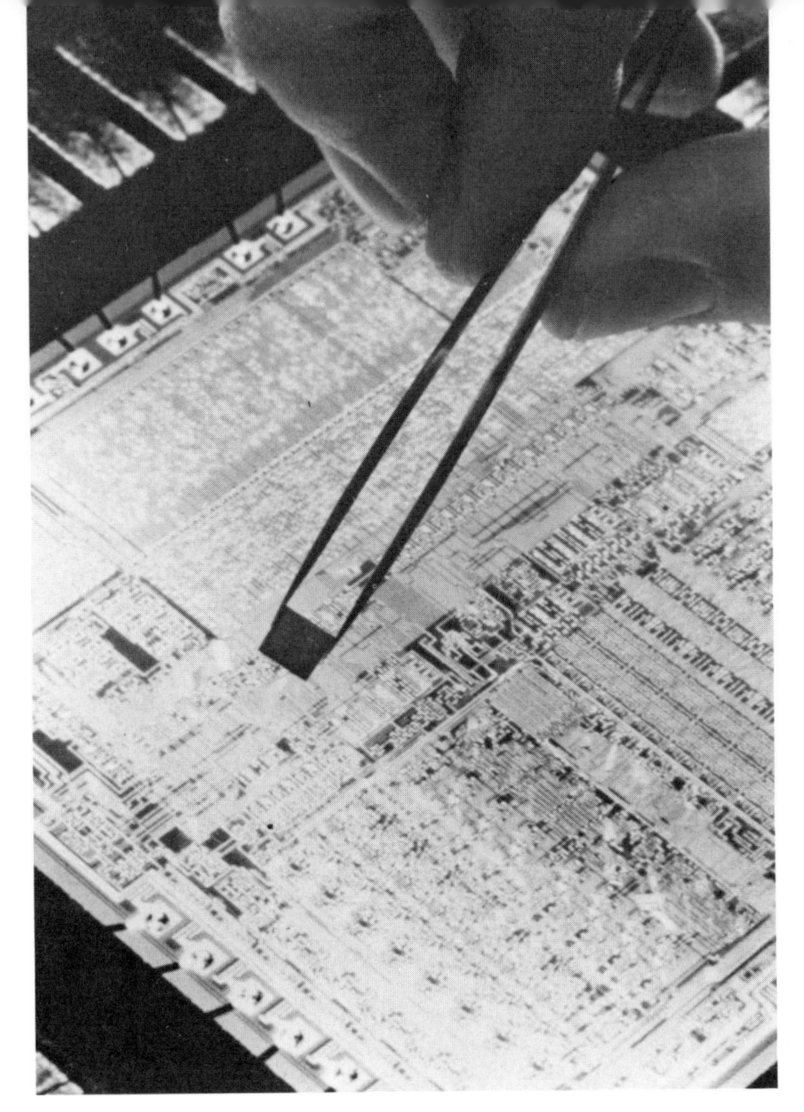

A tiny microprocessor chip takes the place of 7,000 transmitters.

Miniature integrated circuits are also being used to make new kinds of small computers. They are called either microcomputers or microprocessors. All sorts of modern devices, from pocket calculators to automatic cameras to TV games are based on microprocessors.

The future of computers looks very bright indeed. Computer builders are searching for ways to improve their products. Computer experts are finding new uses for this great problem solver. Who knows what uses they will find for a silicon chip that can solve problems in a fraction of a second.

A computerized medical network may be set up to recognize the symptoms and prescribe the treatment for known diseases. A computer attached to your telephone may allow you to send a written letter to distant points on earth in a few seconds. Industrial computers may be used to run the machines in factories so that human workers will be freed from many dull and dangerous jobs.

Fewer errors will be made on future computers. Errors that are made will be easier to correct than today. As more and more people use computers, computers may become as much a part of our lives as television. Some day computers may be as numerous as telephones.

## MEET THE COMPUTER

The computer is an electronic machine. It is a machine that solves problems much as you do. As an example, let's trace the way you would add two numbers. Then, let's see how a computer would do it.

Step 1. You collect information. That is, you either see or hear the numbers to be added.

Step 2. You find a method to solve the problem. In this case, you remember how to do addition.

Step 3. You bring together the information (the two numbers), and the method (addition).

Step 4. You perform the operation, adding the two numbers.

Step 5. You report the results of your work, either by writing down the answer, or by saying it out loud.

All computers go through five similar steps.

Step 1. The computer receives information, or data, from the outside. It changes the data into electronic language, called *input.*

Step 2. The computer has been given a program containing instructions for solving the problem. The instructions are found in the *storage* or memory.

Step 3. The computer brings together the data from the input and the instructions from the storage. This is done by the computer's *control.*

Step 4. The computer goes through the steps of the instructions on the data; this is called *processing.*

Step 5. The computer changes the results from electronic language to human language. It presents the results in print or sound, called *output.*

Sometimes the five parts of a computer—input, storage, control, processor, and output—are together in one large unit. Other times they are far apart and connected by wires. Often, large computers have one control and processing unit, with a number of separate memory, input, and output devices.

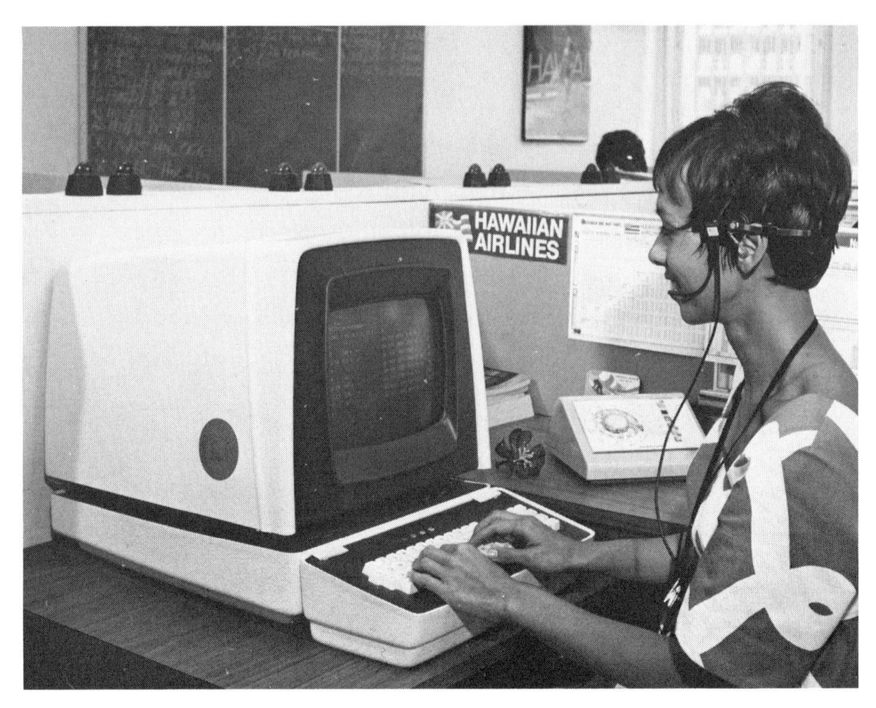


A computer is fed information through the input.

## INPUT: TAKING IN INFORMATION

Computers get most of their input from human beings. Computer operators feed data to the computer through an input device. The most popular input device is the terminal. It looks like an electric typewriter, with a connected television screen.

When you want to enter data into the computer, you type the letters and numbers on the typewriter keyboard. Inside the terminal, the letters and numbers are changed into electrical signals. These signals make up computer language.

Computer language is based on the binary system. It

uses only two symbols, on and off. Either the electricity is flowing or it is not flowing. All the letters and numbers have their own special pattern of ons and offs. It is like the Morse code, which also has only two symbols—dots and dashes—to stand for all the letters and numbers.

The television screen is a cathode ray tube, or CRT. It lets you see, in ordinary letters and numbers, what you are typing into the computer input.

Very often there are several terminals connected to one central processing unit. That lets many people use the central processing unit at the same time. All the terminals used by the tellers in a bank or clerks in an airport, for example, are connected to a central processing unit that may be hundreds of miles away.

Although terminals are very popular, they are not the only input device. Cards, with rows of punched-out holes, can be fed into a machine that reads the pattern of holes, and sends the information, in computer language, to the input. Other devices can actually read printed letters or numbers. Some advanced inputs can even recognize human speech!

Computer experts feed two kinds of information to the computer's input. First, they instruct the computer on how to solve particular problems and perform certain tasks. This is called the computer's program. The program for a bank computer, for instance, instructs the computer on how to keep track of people's accounts, how to add on interest, and how to bring bank books up to date. The program of an airline computer, on the other hand, reserves seats for the different flights, and prints out the tickets.

Second, experts feed the computer the data, the particular facts and figures to be used in its calculations. The bank computer is fed the exact amount of each deposit or withdrawal from an account. And the airline computer is given the name of every passenger that reserves a seat on a plane.

From the input, the program and the data go to the storage part of the computer.

## STORAGE: REMEMBERING FACTS, REMEMBERING METHODS

The program and data are kept in the computer's storage, or memory, until they are needed. Every part of the program and every item of data is stored in a specific place, known as an address. That is how the computer can quickly get back, or retrieve, any bit of information that is needed.

The program and data are kept in the computer's memory.

The core memory has thousands of tiny metal doughnuts strung on thin wires.

Usually the program is kept in the main memory. Until recently, the main memory of most computers used tiny metal doughnuts, called cores. The cores were strung on a grid of criss-crossed wires. Each core was magnetized in one direction or the other. One direction was the same as on. The other direction was the same as off. The entire program and all the data were stored on these magnetized cores.

A more advanced memory system stores the information as electrical charges on tiny silicon chips. Each chip, about one-tenth-of-an-inch-square (0.6 sq. cm), holds about sixty-four thousand on or off electrical charges, called bits. The capacity is expected to become even greater in the future.

The most advanced main memory uses tiny magnetic spots, or bubbles, in a thin film of magnetic material. The bubbles are so small that one million of them could fit on a film the size of a silver dollar! Each bubble is magnetized in one direction or the other to carry the information.

The data fed to a computer are most often stored in a separate memory, called the auxiliary memory section. Usually, this is done by magnetism. The most popular

This enlargement shows a small section of a magnetic bubble memory.

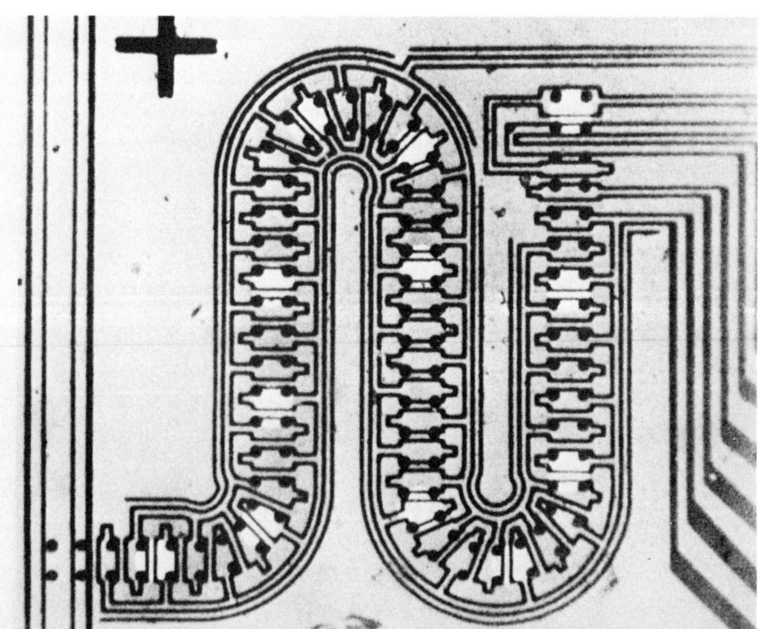

devices are the magnetic tape, magnetic drum, and magnetic disk. In all of these, points on the surface are either magnetized or not. This works the same as electricity on, or electricity off.

## CONTROL: BRINGING INFORMATION TOGETHER

Part of the program of instructions given to a computer goes to the control unit. The control is the traffic cop of the computer.

On the basis of the orders in the program, the control unit decides when to send information from the input to storage and when to send it to the processor. It decides when to call up a program and data from storage. It decides when to accept data from one terminal and when from another terminal. And it decides when the results of the computer's work should go to the output.

In a large computer system, the control and processing units are kept in rows of cabinets.

Just as a good police officer keeps a smooth flow of traffic on a busy road, so a well-programmed control unit keeps a computer working smoothly.

## PROCESSING: DOING THE JOB

The processing section, or the CPU (central processing unit), is the heart of the computer. This section carries out the actual arithmetic and logic tasks. It does all the calculations and makes all the decisions.

Under the direction of the control unit, the CPU adds, subtracts, multiplies, divides, and compares numbers. By combining these basic operations, it does even more complex calculations. The CPU also makes logical decisions. And it does all of these tasks at speeds that are measured in billionths of a second.

Many of the latest CPUs are tiny in size compared to the older ones. They are truly microprocessors. Through the use of microprocessors, it has been possible to increase the number of calculations and add memories to the new computers, without adding to their size or cost.

## OUTPUT: PRESENTING THE RESULTS

The output is the last step in computer operation. It changes the computer's results from binary machine language into a form that people can understand. There

The output of a computer is the part that presents the results.

are several kinds of output devices.

Suppose a shoe store owner wants to know which style of shoe is selling best. He uses a printer. It actually prints, or types, the numbers of shoes sold on a long strip of paper. The computer print-out shows him which shoes he should order. High-speed printers can print an entire line at one time, turning out as many as 20,000 lines a minute.

A city planner, though, may use her computer in a different way. She wants to plan a new bus route to serve the largest number of people. Using a plotter as the output, she gets a drawing, actually a map, showing the route chosen by the computer.

The telephone operator who looks up telephone numbers uses a computer. But she does not need a printed copy, nor a drawing of the number. Therefore, she has a computer terminal with a CRT. The screen flashes the number for a little while, and then it disappears, ready for the next request.

Students in many schools are taught by a computer. Some of these courses are in foreign languages. To learn a language, you must hear it spoken correctly. These computers have an audio output. They actually produce the sounds of the language perfectly pronounced.

The modern computer is truly an amazing machine. But it is not able to think for itself. It is only as smart as the person who prepares its program. Nor can a computer produce correct answers unless it is fed correct data.

Many people are a little afraid of computers. They think of computers as machines with minds of their own. Just remember this, though. A computer is nothing more than a human tool. It stretches our abilities. Just as you use a hammer to help you drive a nail into a wall, so you use a computer to help you solve a problem. Computers are our servants, not our masters.

# 3 MAKING PEOPLE WELL

## HEART DISEASE

A forty-seven-year-old man arrives at the hospital with terrible pains in his chest. He is rushed to the cardiology unit, the part of the hospital that treats heart disease.

The nurses place him on an examining table. The table is in the middle of a room that contains advanced electronic equipment and a modern computer to help diagnose heart disease. Speedy diagnosis may mean the difference between life and death.

A nurse gives the patient an injection in his arm. The injected substance is known to attach itself only to healthy heart cells. Then she lowers a device, called a gamma scintillation camera, over his chest. The gamma scintillation camera follows the movement of the substance in his body.

The camera is connected to the input of the computer. The computer produces a color picture of the man's heart

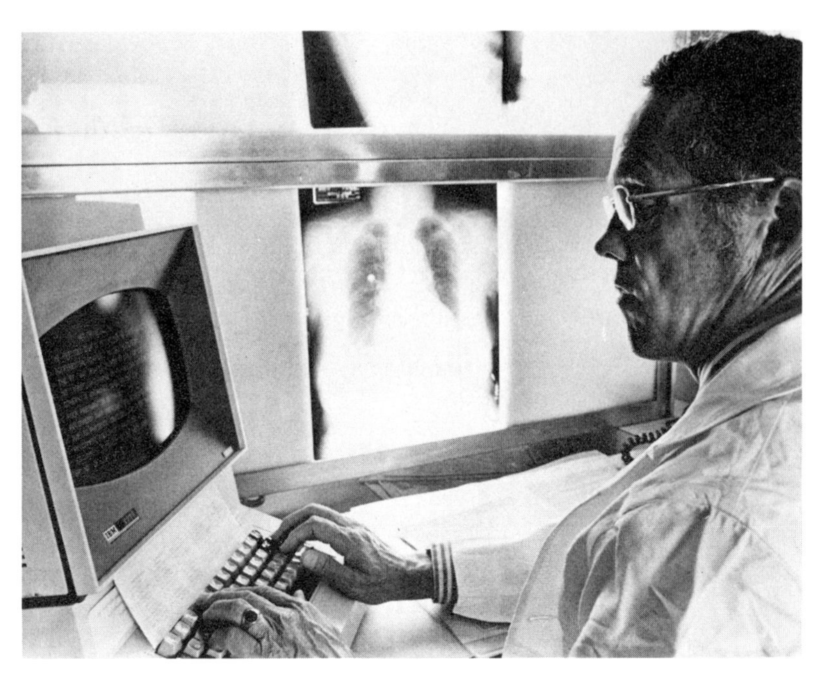

More and more doctors are using computers in the practice of medicine.

A computer system keeps track of the condition of a very sick patient.

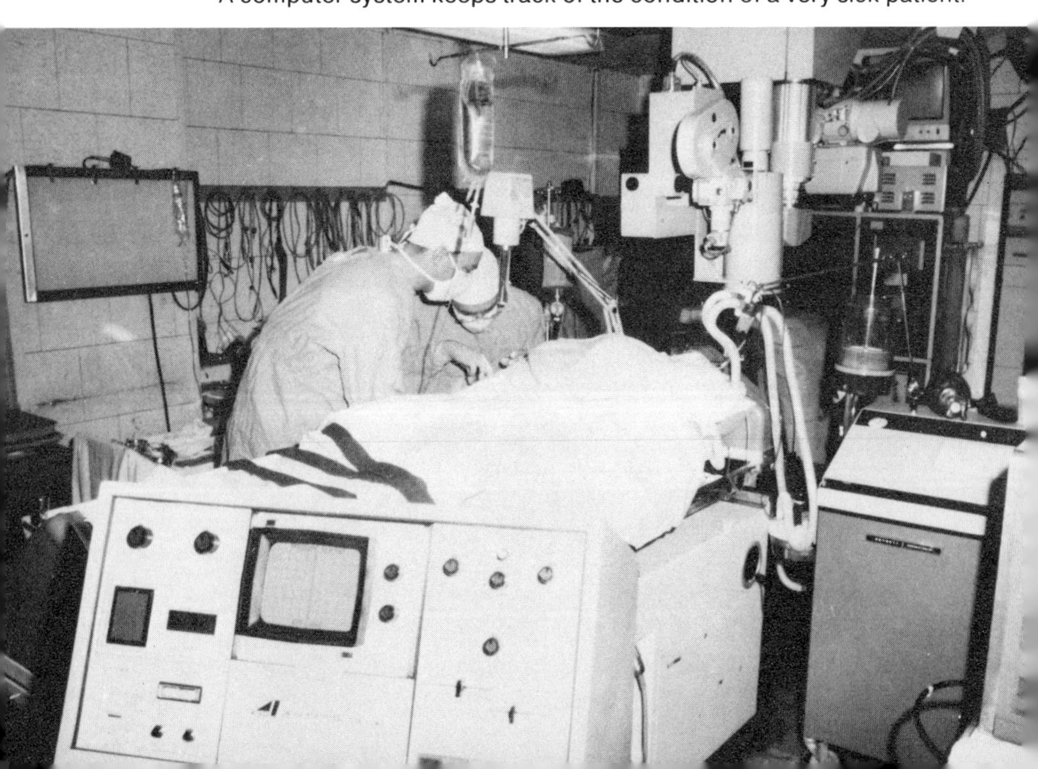

on the CRT. The healthy areas are light in color. The damaged areas are dark.

A team of doctors watches the patient's heart on the CRT. They see that his heart is not pumping the way it should. The patient has indeed suffered a heart attack. Based on the picture of his heart in action, the doctors decide on the best treatment.

As soon as his condition is stable, the patient is taken to a regular hospital room. A number of wires attached to his body measure his heartbeat, his blood pressure, and his temperature. They are all connected to a computer.

The computer monitors, or keeps track of, his condition. It is programmed with the normal range of figures for these vital functions. If any measurement goes outside these limits, the computer sounds a warning signal. This alerts the nurse. At the same time, the output printer of the computer makes a permanent record of the results. Doctors judge the patient's condition by studying the print-out.

Within a few days, the man is better. The doctors run some computerized tests that measure the flow of blood in his body. The computer figures help the doctors plan any further treatment that is needed.

Another heart patient, a young woman, is helped by a computer monitor in her home, many miles from the hospital. She has a pacemaker that keeps her heart beating at a steady rate. From time to time, though, the doctors want to check that the pacemaker is working correctly, and that her heartbeat is normal.

For these checks, the patient puts in a telephone call to the hospital's computer. She holds a small box on her chest and places the telephone receiver on top of the box. The box picks up signals from both the pacemaker and from the heartbeat.

The signals go out over the telephone line to the computer. The computer's processing unit compares the signals from the pacemaker with a record of signals made earlier and stored in the computer's memory. The computer prints out the figures. They help the doctors decide whether or not the woman needs to come to the hospital for an examination. Either way, the results are stored in the memory of the computer for future use.

## KIDNEY TRANSPLANT

Tuesday, June 26, 1979: A fourteen-year-old girl in Norfolk, Virginia, dies at noon as the result of head injuries suffered in an auto accident. A hospital official asks the girl's parents to donate her kidneys for transplants in patients with kidney disease. They agree. The kidneys are removed from the girl's body and tested for blood type.

Kidneys can only be kept for seventy-two hours. The doctors quickly call the other hospitals in Norfolk. They are looking for patients with the same blood type who are awaiting a transplant. No luck.

They call the office of a computer network in Richmond, Virginia. The computer holds in its memory a list of all kidney patients in the southeastern United States who are awaiting kidney transplants. The computer locates a patient in Newark, New Jersey. The doctors wrap the kidneys, pack them in ice, and place them on a midnight plane to Newark.

Wednesday, June 27, 1979: Early in the morning, the girl's right kidney is transplanted into the body of the Newark man. The operation is a success, and the man's life is saved, helped in part by the vast memory and great speed of the computer.

## PATIENT DIAGNOSIS

At Beth Israel Hospital in Boston a computer takes a patient's history before he or she sees the doctor. This saves the doctor time. It also lets the patient think about answers without feeling rushed. And some patients feel more comfortable talking to a computer rather than to a doctor.

The person sits at a computer terminal. The computer presents the questions on a CRT. The patient types in the answers on a keyboard.

At the end of the interview, the computer prints out a summary of the patient's answers. The doctor uses the summary to ask the patient further questions, and to determine the type of examination.

At Beth Israel and other hospitals there are computers

programmed with long lists of diseases, and their symptoms. The doctors key in the symptoms, such as headaches, pain in legs, rash on back, or loss of appetite. Then the computer searches through its memory to find the disease or diseases with these symptoms. The computer also suggests further questions to ask, or tests to perform.

The use of computers to diagnose conditions believed to be related to the brain is known as neurometrics. Recently it was used to diagnose the condition of a six-year-old boy named Chris.

Chris was not as active as other children his age. He had difficulty in learning to walk, and was very late in starting to speak. Yet doctors could not find anything wrong with him.

Chris was given the neurometric tests. Doctors placed nineteen electrodes around the outside of his head. They were connected to the computer. The electrodes picked up tiny electrical signals from Chris's brain, and sent them to a computer.

The computer sampled the results from each electrode two hundred times a second. In one minute, it collected over two hundred thousand bits of information.

These figures were compared with standard, normal figures stored in the computer's memory. Study of the results showed that mentally Chris was far below average in certain areas. He was suffering from a condition similar to epilepsy. The doctors prescribed some drugs to control his problem. The medicine, along with special methods of education, have helped Chris get along much better than before.

## TREATING DISABILITIES

An eight-year-old girl in Florida almost never speaks. She hardly seems to notice other people. Withdrawn and alone most of the time, she just sits and rocks back and forth.

The girl's doctor is using a computer to help communicate with her. The child sits at a computer terminal and pushes a key. A picture of a dog appears on the screen. A recorded voice says, "dog." Pushing different keys brings up other pictures and other words. It becomes a sort of game. Although it does not involve others, it is fun for her and she is learning new words. Maybe, in time, it will help her to begin to talk to others.

At the University of Wisconsin Medical School, a computer is better able to predict when a patient will attempt suicide than a psychiatrist.

In one test, a group of seventy-two patients were interviewed by the computer. The computer predicted that three of the patients would try to take their own lives. The psychiatrist predicted that none would.

Within forty-eight hours, the three patients did attempt suicide. Over a nine-month period, the computer identified ninety percent of those who later tried to commit suicide. The psychiatrist only identified thirty percent.

Why did the computer do better than a trained doctor? Perhaps because patients often hesitate to tell others about feeling that they are ashamed of. They are afraid that people will not approve, and will show anger, disgust or pity.

The computer does not react. It is completely impersonal. And it is able to get honest answers to even a blunt question such as: "Are you planning to kill yourself?"

Psychiatrists are also using the computer to improve their skill in diagnosing mental illness. A psychiatrist was once seated at a computer terminal. She was told that a patient was at another terminal in a different room. The psychiatrist was able to ask the patient any questions she wanted.

The conversation began like this:

Doctor: Hello. My name is Dr. Jones.

Patient: Hello. I am Pat Smith.

Doctor: How do you feel?

Patient: I'm upset today.

Doctor: Why are you upset?

Patient: It's my job. I just can't get ahead.

Doctor: Why?

Patient: My boss hates me.

Doctor: Is it anything you did?

Patient: No. Everyone at work hates me.

Doctor: Do you think a psychiatrist could help you?

Patient: No. No. A psychiatrist would lock me up.

At the end of a long interview, the psychiatrist said that Pat Smith seemed to be suffering from paranoia. This is a condition in which patients believe that everyone is trying to harm them. The doctor had no reason to believe she was not talking with Pat Smith.

Later, the psychiatrist was told that she had been having a conversation with a computer. The computer was programmed to answer questions just like a typical patient suffering from paranoia.

One mentally ill patient was so afraid of people that he refused to speak. His psychiatrist seated him at a computer terminal. He told the patient to type messages into the computer. The hope was that it would be easier for him to talk to a machine than to a person.

The psychiatrist went to a computer terminal in another room. The psychiatrist "spoke" with the man via computer. After five days, the man was ready to speak to the psychiatrist face-to-face.

Computers will, of course, never take the place of doctors, psychiatrists, and nurses. But they are already helping these professionals to diagnose and treat many different medical conditions.

# 4 SENDING AND GETTING MESSAGES

## THE NEW VIDEO

A young mother in Ohio goes to college, but she never leaves her home. She sees and hears the professor on her own television set. Connected to the TV set is a hand-held key pad that looks like a modern calculator. She answers the teacher's questions by pressing the various push buttons. Only once, for the final exam, does she go to the college itself.

A lawyer suddenly finds she must fly to Chicago to see a client. She turns on her TV set and presses some buttons on her telephone. In seconds, the schedule of flights to Chicago appears on the screen. She reserves a seat by pressing several of the telephone's buttons.

A farmer gets the latest weather and crop information. A doctor looks over reports on patients' conditions from the medical lab. An investor receives the latest stock market reports. A home buyer sees an up-to-date list of houses for sale. A shopper checks the items on sale at the supermarket.

These people are all part of a test being run in Ohio, Florida, Utah, Missouri, and Washington, D.C., of a new computer-television system known as Videotex. Videotex turns your home television set into a computer terminal.

There are two basic approaches to Videotex. One system, called Prestel or Viewdata, uses regular telephone lines to bring the data into your home. To use Prestel, you turn on your special TV set. Then you press a button on the small key pad to reach the Prestel center by telephone. You press other buttons to call up the exact data you want, which appear on the TV screen.

Prestel is receiving its biggest test in Great Britain. Fifteen hundred TV sets in London are able to receive Prestel's signal. These sets cost quite a bit more than ordinary sets; a color set runs about $2,000. Additional electronic equipment is also needed to link the TV to the telephone, and to decode the computer signal.

The British Prestel system has some two hundred thousand "pages" of information in its memory. A page is all the printed material that can be displayed at one time on a TV screen. More data, however, are always being added. The goal is to have nine million pages of information. At the moment there is a charge of about ten cents for each page of data called up.

Prestel users may buy items from store catalogs, make travel arrangements, reserve theater seats, and transfer money from bank accounts through the system. Special code numbers even allow users to send messages to each other.

The other system, Teletext, depends only on your TV set, without the telephone. A TV picture is made up of 504 separate lines. There are another 21 lines that are not needed for TV broadcasting. Under the Teletext system, a central computer transmits its data over the 21 unused lines.

As with Prestel, the viewer punches in various signals on a hand-held key pad. The material then appears on the screen instead of the regular broadcast. The same wide range of information and data can be called up on the television screen.

Teletext can be received on any TV set, as long as you have a decoder. A decoder can be added to a new set at the factory for about fifty dollars. It costs about one hundred fifty dollars to install one on an old set. Under the present plan, the data from Teletext is free. The costs are met by advertisers who put ads on the data pages.

The Teletext system has some drawbacks. Data can only be sent out by the broadcasting companies while they are on the air. It has room for no more than eight hundred pages of data in its memory. And there is no way to communicate from one set to another.

Video information systems are surely here to stay. There is some doubt, though, about which system will become the most popular and widely accepted. The manufacturers and the public are watching and waiting to see how the combination of computers and television works out.

## TELEPHONE

Do you ever call long distance from a pay phone?

You dial the number, and then you hear something like: "Sixty cents, please. Please deposit sixty cents for the first three minutes."

If you are placing the call in New York State, don't try to ask the operator a question. There is no one on the line with you. The voice you hear comes from a computer. It has a vocabulary of seventy words in its memory. This program is known as the Automatic Coin Telephone Service.

The words and numbers are first recorded, each word and number by itself, by an actress. The sounds are then changed into electronic signals and stored in a computer memory circuit. The circuit is hooked into the computer that controls all the calls made from pay telephones.

While you dial your call, the computer senses each of the numbers. When you finish, it calculates the cost, and produces the voice that you hear. As soon as you deposit the money, the computer automatically connects your call.

Have you ever called information and heard an operator say: "Information. May I help you?"

You tell the operator a name and he or she gives you

Computers make the job of the telephone information operator faster and easier.

the phone number. In the past, the operator would have to thumb through the telephone directory to look up the number. Now, a new computer system provides this information much more quickly. Sometimes it can find the number even if you misspell the name.

Information operators who use this new system type in the name you give on the computer terminal. In a flash, the computer displays the name and telephone number on the CRT. At the same time, the computer calls up nine similar names. In case you spelled the name wrong, the operator may still be able to find it.

All new phones are also entered into this computer

A computerized electronic system connects the telephones each time you make a call. It is also used to test the lines.

system. The information operators, therefore, have the up-to-the-minute listings. At the end of the year, the computer is hooked to a machine that automatically sets the type for the new telephone directory. The directory is then printed from this type—accurately, quickly, and at a great savings in cost.

Have you ever made a long distance call, and not been able to hear the person at the other end?

Usually, something is wrong with the electronic circuit on that line. Telephone companies used to make test calls on each of the lines about once a week. Now the testing of lines is done largely by computers. The computer system tests each trunk line from two to twenty times a day, and at a fraction of the cost.

The computer makes a print-out for each line. It shows the expected sound volume, and the actual volume. It calculates the percentage of lines below standard volume, and the average time it takes them to fall below standard. Engineers then use this information to plan a maintenance program that will prevent failures before they occur.

## MAIL

Until recently, there were two basic ways to send a message to another person. You could send a letter. This method is slow, but the other person ends up with a piece of paper, called a hard copy, which bears the message. Or you could use the telephone. The telephone is fast, but there is no hard copy.

The newest way to send messages combines mail and telephone. It is called electronic mail. As fast as a phone call, it provides the same hard copy as a letter sent through the mail.

There are several ways to send hard copy by electronic mail. You can send messages electronically by teletype. The teletype machine looks like an electric typewriter. As you type letters or numbers on the teletype, the machine changes them into electronic signals. The signals pass through telephone wires connected to another teletype machine located somewhere else. When the electronic signals arrive, the receiving machine actually types out the message. Thus, within minutes, the original message appears on the other teletype.

A facsimile machine, or "fax," is like the teletype. But with the fax you place the letter directly into the machine. The machine changes the letter—whether it be words, numbers, drawings, or photographs—into electronic signals. The signals then pass through the wires to other fax machines.

Computers are attached to some fax machines to add special features. The computers can adjust the electronic signals in order to send messages from one fax machine to a receiving fax machine made by a different company. Computers attached to some fax machines can even tell the user how they should be operated. Thus you do not need special training to send out messages.

One transmission can send the same message to any number of receivers. Some fax machines are able to store up messages. It is therefore possible to send out messages at night, when the rates for telephone lines are lower, and have them read the next morning.

One form of electronic mail uses neither teletype nor facsimile. This system hooks up computer-to-computer. The message goes directly from the output of one computer into the input of another. This is a particularly useful way to transfer great amounts of information.

Teletype, facsimile and computer-to-computer forms

of electronic mail are excellent, fast, and reliable ways to send hard copy messages from one place to another. But they all need special equipment to send and receive these messages.

The U.S. Postal Service is now testing a different approach to electronic mail. It is called ECOM (Electronic Computer-Originated Mail). Here is how it works: suppose you want to send a message from Dallas to Chicago by ECOM. You take the message to a nearby communication company office, and a worker feeds your message into a teletype, a fax, or a computer. From this office, the electronic signal passes to the regional post office closest to the Chicago address. A printout of the message appears there, and is delivered along with the other mail.

At present, ECOM is mainly used by companies that send out large numbers of bills that they want to have arrive quickly. Credit card, telephone, and electric bills are some examples. Other businesses, though, are beginning to find ways to use ECOM.

It costs about $1.25 to send a message by electronic mail today. The cost will probably drop by about 25 percent a year as the volume of users picks up and the technology improves. In time, electronic mail may completely replace the old-fashioned letter.

## NEWSPAPERS

Newspaper offices used to be noisy, busy places. Reporters would dash in with their notes. They would sit down at their typewriters, and make a great clatter as they typed out their articles. When finished they would shout, "Copy!" A young copy boy would pick up the story, and take it to the editor. Often the editor would yell questions across the room to reporters. They would bark back their answers.

The edited story was taken to the linotype operators. These workers sat at monster machines that created lines of metal type. The lines of type were than made into full pages and sent to the pressroom to be printed.

Today's newspaper offices are very different. They are quiet. The floors are carpeted. There is hardly a typewriter to be seen or heard. Reporters and editors sit at separate computer terminals. Each one has a typewriter keyboard and a CRT screen, which they call VDT (Video Display Terminal).

The reporters type their stories on the silent electronic keyboards of the computer terminals. The words go into the computer memory. They also appear as small green figures on the VDT. By pushing various keys, a reporter can rewrite sentences, correct misspellings, and even move whole paragraphs. When the story is finished, the reporter pushes a button. The story goes into the computer's memory until the editor is ready to see it.

The editors call up the stories from the computer memory by pressing certain keys on their terminals. They read the stories on their VDTs, making any cuts or changes that are needed. Once the stories are set, they strike another key. This starts the stories through the automatic process that ends with a metal printing plate. The plates then go to the pressroom where the newspaper is printed.

## LIBRARIES

Libraries all over the country are switching to computer check-out. To make the changeover, clerks sit at rows of computer terminals. Behind them are carts of books.

One at a time, they pick up the books and paste a "zebra label" into each one. The label has a pattern of thick and thin black lines with numbers underneath them. It looks like the zebra label found on so many supermarket items.

The clerks then key the information into the computer: author, title, publisher, date, cost, and zebra number. When they finish, all the thousands of books in the library will have zebra labels, and will be entered into the computer's memory. The library's circulation system will then be run by the computer.

Do you want to borrow a book from the computerized library of the future?

Bring your book and library card to the front desk. The clerk places your card in the computer checkout terminal. Then he or she slides the book's zebra label through the laser reader. In a fraction of a second the book is checked out to you.

At the same time, though, the computer checks your

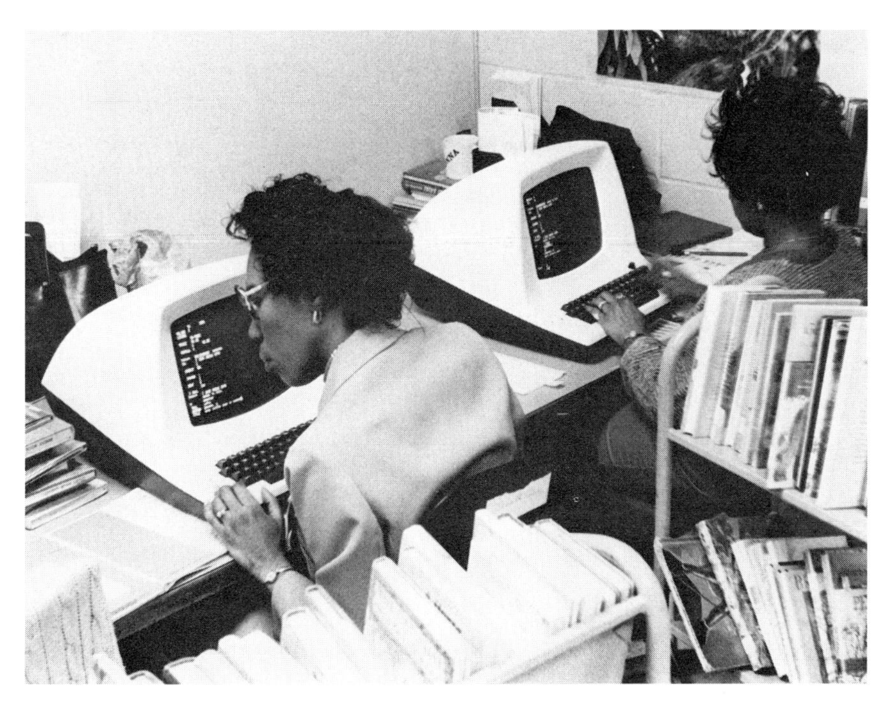

Clerks at a library enter information on each book into a computer.

card number through its memory. Do you have any books out that are overdue? Do you owe the library any fines? Do you have more books out on loan than the limit allows? The computer signals the clerk if it finds any of these problems.

Is a certain book that you want missing from the shelf?

The computer quickly checks the records. If someone has checked it out, the computer notes when it is due back. It puts a reserve on the book in your name. If not, the computer lets you know that the book is in the library, and you can look again.

Do you need information for a school report?

You sit at a computer terminal. Quickly and easily you call up complete lists of books and magazine articles on the subject. This saves the time and effort of thumbing through the card catalog and looking through other lists of books and articles.

Are you looking for a book that your library does not own?

All of the library computers in an area are connected, so the computer can search for the book in the other libraries. If it finds a copy, it arranges to have the book delivered to your library so that you can borrow it.

The computerized library also helps librarians. They are able to locate any book in a moment. A computer print-out shows how many times each book has been borrowed. The librarians are able to use these figures to order more of the popular books. The computer is even able to send out overdue notices.

# 5 GETTING FROM PLACE TO PLACE

## AUTOMOBILES

The Ford Motor Company uses more than one hundred separate computers. Most of them are used in data processing. They do everything from ordering supplies to paying salaries, from sending out bills to preparing sales figures.

But one very important use of computers is in designing and testing new cars and car parts. In the past manufacturers used the old "cut and try" method. The car designers built models of the car or part, then had it tested or driven.

This is how the new, computerized design method works: first the computer is fed all the information on the size and shape of the car. It also holds information on how the different parts work. How long is the body? Is the trunk edge straight or curved? How do the brakes work on each wheel? What happens when you step on the gas?

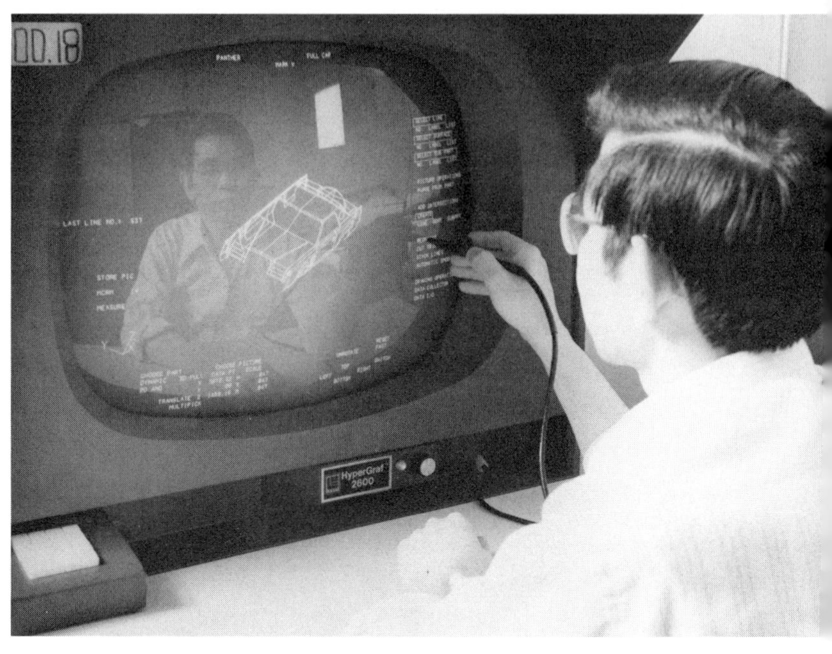


Automobile designers use computers to plan new cars.

Once this information is locked into the computer's memory, the engineers start to design new and better parts and systems for the car.

Let's say an engineer is working on a new design for the hood of a car. The engineer feeds the new design into the computer. The computer puts it in place on the car that is already in its memory. It then displays the car, with the new hood, on the CRT.

The engineer sees how it looks. He or she can turn the image around to see it from different angles. The engineer shines a light pen into the CRT to make changes in the design. Will the new hood be strong enough for the use it will have? Will it open and close easily? Will it block the driver's view of the street? These are some

The computerized Alpha 3-D has a probe that moves over any surface. It can then make a copy of that same surface.

of the questions the computer is able to answer.

One computer program is set up to show what will happen when a particular car part is put under pressure. The part itself is shown in blue. The computer program then increases the stress on the part. Where the pressure is greatest, the part turns red. This helps the engineer to decide if the part should be stronger, and which points are weakest.

The Ford Motor Company also has a computer-controlled machine known as Alpha 3-D. Alpha 3-D has a probe that skims over the surface of any object. It can describe every part of the car, from an engine to a door. Even the whole auto can be covered. The exact location of every point goes into the computer's memory. The engineer then directs the computer either to show the outline of the object on the CRT, or to prepare an ink drawing. A machine tool is connected to Alpha 3-D. Under the control of the computer it can shape and build either a small-scale or a full-sized model of the part or of the car.

The best car engines are those that go the most miles on a gallon of gasoline without adding to air pollution. These engines burn just the right amount of fuel at exactly the right time in the engine's cycle.

But how do you control the engine so that it runs at peak performance all the time? It is impossible to carry a mechanic under the hood to adjust the engine as you drive. But some auto makers have found that a microcomputer can do the job.

The input to these computers comes from sensors. These devices measure the way the engine performs. As the car is driven they take readings on the heat, speed, position of the engine parts, amount of oxygen in the exhaust gas, outside temperature, and a number of other factors. These measurements are received by the computer as electric signals.

The computer processes the information at the rate of several million calculations per second. It compares the way the car is running with standard figures already in its memory, to determine if the engine is running as well as possible.

Through electronic controls, the computer makes any

changes in the engine that are necessary. It may adjust the ratio of air to fuel. It may change the firing speed of the spark plugs. It may send more exhaust gas back to be burned again. This goes on all the time, without stopping and without errors.

Since 1980, Cadillac has been putting microcomputers into a number of its cars. The dashboard display lets the drivers know how many miles to a gallon they are getting. On long trips it also tells them how far they have gone, the distance they have yet to go, and when they will arrive.

Volkswagen is testing a new computer system that will give drivers even more information. For this test, special wires were buried in the ground beneath six main roads in Germany.

The underground wires sense the flow of traffic on the roads. They are connected to a computer in a central office. Information from the wires goes into the computer. The computer then notes where the traffic is moving well and where there are traffic jams.

At the start of a trip, the driver keys in the destination on the car's computer. As the car passes over the buried wires, the computer signals the car's destination. In return, the underground wires send back instructions on the fastest way to go. These are shown as simple line maps on the computer screen.

About two hundred cities in the United States have computerized traffic lights. The typical system has sensors buried in the road. These magnetic devices sense the movement of cars and trucks.

The sensors feed the information to a central computer. In some cities, the sensors are connected to the computer by telephone lines. In a few cities, the information is beamed on laser light from the sensor to the computer. Engineers have found that sometimes the laser can be cheaper than telephone lines. The computer processes the figures of the traffic flow. It adjusts the traffic lights to move the greatest volume of traffic in the fastest possible way.

Traffic flows much faster with computerized traffic control. It saves time and fuel, and cuts the number of accidents. Also, by reducing the number of traffic jams, it reduces the pollution caused by cars.

The city of Tokyo, Japan, has some of the worst traffic troubles in the world. All traffic just about comes to a halt during the evening rush hours, from about 3:30 to 7:00 P.M. To help ease the problem, the Tokyo Metropolitan Police Department is using an advanced system of computerized traffic control.

Thirty-two microphones hang over major roads in the city. They are the electronic "ears" of the system. They pick up the sound waves of the passing cars. They send the information to a computer. The computer calculates how much traffic is moving on each roadway. It automatically adjusts the traffic signals to get the best possible flow.

Tokyo, which has some of the worst traffic jams in the world, uses an advanced system of computerized traffic control.

Twenty TV cameras watch the busiest traffic intersections. They are the electronic "eyes" of the system. The television cameras are also plugged into the computer to provide more information on how to keep the traffic moving.

Computer operators in the traffic control center watch about a dozen receivers that show the pictures from the TV cameras. They are on the lookout for accidents. They can quickly send out emergency help. If necessary, they override the computer, and change the signals to break up a bad traffic snarl.

The computer system not only controls the three thousand traffic lights in Tokyo, but it also flashes messages on electronic signboards along the roads. These bulletins tell drivers about traffic conditions. They suggest different routes in case there is a tie-up.

## AIRPLANES

The pilot of the 747 jet approaches San Francisco. He can make out the Golden Gate Bridge. Soon he sees the lights of the airport. Gently he brings the plane down on the runway. The airport buildings flash by on either side as he speeds along.

All at once, the captain sees the glaring lights of another plane. It is heading across his path. Quickly he yanks back on the stick. The 747 lurches, and rises up again. He narrowly avoids the accident. The pilot circles the field once more. This time he comes in for a perfect landing.

When the pilot leaves the cockpit he is laughing and joking. This may seem like a strange way to act after a nearly fatal crash. But it is not really surprising. Although the pilot went through all the steps of landing at San Francisco, he never left the ground!

The pilot was seated in a model of the cockpit of the 747. A computer created the CRT views of the airport.

This is the pilot's view from the cockpit of a DC-10 in a computerized training system.

The computer changed the picture to agree with the speed he was flying. It sent a picture of the other plane into view. And if he had not been fast enough, it would have shown a tremendous crash and explosion.

VITAL (Virtual Image Takeoff and Landing) is a popular computerized pilot training system. The CRT display of VITAL is mounted on the windows of the model cockpit. All the pilot can see is images of the airport, the nearby cities, and the countryside. It shows buildings, roads, hills, and rivers. It can be daylight, twilight, or night; clear, foggy, or raining; above the clouds, inside the clouds, or beneath the clouds. For night views there are up to eight thousand lights showing airport lights, city lights, highway lights, and the lights of moving traffic.

As the pilot lands or takes off, the computer changes the image thirty times per second. It shows how the view changes during actual flight. Also, the computer memory can hold the information on up to fifty different airports!

Computerized pilot training gives the pilots many hours of training without the danger and expense of actually flying the planes. It allows them to become familiar with airports all over the world. It gives them practice in flying under various conditions. And it gives them the opportunity to face and handle all sorts of emergencies.

Pilot training is just one small part of the airlines' use of computers. The biggest use is in making reservations. Every time you buy an airline ticket, the sale goes through the computer system.

United Airlines has one of the biggest computer systems. It is known as Apollo. The main Apollo computer is in Denver, Colorado. There is also a network of about sixteen thousand computer terminals from coast to coast.

At any moment, the giant memory of the Apollo system includes information on some 2 million reservations. Every day it answers about 5 million questions. It gives nearly 700,000 ticket prices. During the same day, the computer also makes around 128,000 new reservations, prints out some 80,000 tickets, and makes roughly 5,000 car rentals.

Just before takeoff, the latest weather along the route is fed into the computer. The passenger list and the amount of cargo is also added to the computer's input. Within seconds, the computer processes all this information. It calculates the best route, speed, and altitude for the greatest safety and fuel economy, and earliest time of arrival. Computers help to guide the planes as well.

## AIR TRAFFIC CONTROL

It is one hour before the take-off of TWA Flight 7 from New York to Los Angeles. TWA files its flight plans with the New York Air Traffic Control Center. While the passengers are boarding the plane, the computers at the Center check the flight plan to make sure that the flight will not be near any other scheduled flights. The plan is cleared. The computers give the pilot the go ahead.

At departure time, the pilot radios the airport Control Tower for instructions. The air traffic controllers guide the plane out to the runway. After a few minutes, they give the pilot clearance for takeoff. As soon as the plane is in the air, the radar and radio beacons of the Air Traffic Control start to track the flight.

The radar antenna sends out continuous radio signals over a two hundred mile circle in the sky. When the signals strike an object, such as a plane, they are reflected back to the antenna. The length of time it takes the signal to go back and forth, and the direction the antenna is facing, determine the plane's location. The radar is also able to find the plane's speed of flight.

At the same time, a coded radio beacon is beamed up into the sky from the ground. This beam strikes an electronic device on the plane, called a transponder. The transponder automatically sends out a signal. The signal identifies the plane and gives its height from the ground, or altitude.

The data from the radar antenna and from the radio beacon go to the Air Traffic Control computers. The computers analyze the information. They display the plane as a dot, known as a blip, on the computer screen. Alongside the blip, the computers show the airline and flight number, the assigned altitude, the actual altitude, and the plane's code number.

TWA Flight 7 heads west. It comes to the boundary of the New York sector. Already the flight plan has been relayed to the next sector, the Cleveland sector. When it is close to the boundary, flashing lights on the screen warn Cleveland Air Traffic Control that the flight is entering its air space.

The Cleveland computers check to make sure that there is space for the plane. If there is, the flight is allowed to cross into the Cleveland sector. If the plane's route takes it too near another plane, the computers trigger a "conflict alert." Lights flash on the controllers' screens, warning them of the danger. It gives them time to direct one of the pilots to change course.

In this way, TWA Flight 7 is handed from sector to sector until it approaches Los Angeles. About fifty miles from Los Angeles, control passes to the airport tower, which brings the plane in for a safe landing.

New computer systems are being developed to make air traffic control even safer and more reliable. One system provides both controllers and pilots with computer display screens showing nearby traffic. The computer gives directions on how to avert danger. But both the pilot and the controller can override the computer if they see a better solution. Another system is based on the comparison of the actual flight route with the flight plan. If the pilot strays too far, a warning sounds in the cockpit of the plane.

## MARINE RESEARCH

CAORF (Computer Aided Operations Research Facility) is a computer research simulator at the Merchant Marine Research Center in Kings Point, New York.

CAORF does for ship captains what VITAL does for

The captain stands on the make-believe bridge of a ship. He can see a computerized display of other ships moving by.

airplane pilots. That is, the CAORF computer gives captains the illusion that they are sailing ships, just as VITAL gives pilots the illusion that they are flying planes. The difference is that CAORF is used mostly for research, VITAL for training.

One recent CAORF project concerned the harbor at Valdez, Alaska. This harbor was going to be used for the first time by giant oil supertankers. How should the tankers enter and leave the harbor? Where should they be loaded with the oil? What would happen if a sudden wind came up while the ship was steaming out of the

Each "voyage" at the National Maritime Research Center is directed from the Control Center.

harbor? If the ship lost power? If the rudder gave way? At CAORF the researchers studied the situation so that they could give suggestions on building the harbor facilities, and give instructions on how to sail big ships in and out.

Within the building that houses the CAORF computer is a realistic copy of the bridge found on today's large oil tankers or freighters. It has all the controls found on a typical ship. When a captain looks out through the windows, he sees the water, other ships, and views of the land and buildings around the harbor or waterway.

While it all looks very real, he is seeing a full-color changing picture. It is flashed onto a large screen by five television projectors.

The computer's data base contains information both on ships and on harbors and waterways. How do ships move through the water? How do they change speed and direction? How are they affected by winds, currents, tides, and water depths? What happens with ships of different length and weight? The information on harbors includes their shape and size, depth, usual winds and tides, and typical traffic patterns. To this is added the sights a sailor would notice in the harbor—the bridges and docks on the water, the big buildings and landmarks on shore.

To do the Valdez research, the computer was programmed to move like a 250,000 ton (226,800 metric tons) supertanker in the harbor. A captain was then asked to take the ship out to sea. As the captain sailed along, everything looked as it would in Valdez harbor. All the sights and landmarks were there. And as the captain moved the ship through the harbor, the views changed with changes in the ship's speed and position.

While the captain ran the ship, the operators in charge of the experiment sat in the computer control room. They followed the movements of the ship on computer screens. They created many different conditions. It was night time; only pinpoints of light could be seen. They made a thunderstorm; bolts of lightning and heavy rains appeared.

The captain had to depend on radar. How well does it work in this situation? The operators sent another ship across the screen, heading for a collision. Could the captain avoid the collision? They whipped up powerful winds that pushed against the ship. Could the captain keep control? They made believe there was a loss of power, a broken rudder, powerful tides, radio failure, and other emergencies. Was the captain able to prevent serious accidents?

Throughout these tests, TV cameras and tape recorders were watching and listening to the captain. An important part of the research at CAORF is concerned with how humans behave while facing difficult situations on board a ship.

Psychologists studied the captain's behavior. Later, they would use their findings to suggest new equipment and new designs to help sea captains. What were the moments and situations of greatest stress? How could they ease them or take them away?

In the past, there were only two ways to find out about using a new harbor. You could send ships into the actual harbor, and see what happened. Or, you could guess what would happen.

Now, with CAORF, you don't have to take such risks. The computers show just what can happen as you sail all kinds of ships through all sorts of harbors.

# 6 WORKING IN BUSINESS AND INDUSTRY

## SUPERMARKETS

Many people complain about shopping in supermarkets. The store is sometimes out of the product they are looking for. They have to stand in line to get their vegetables weighed and to get checks approved. And finally, they have to wait in long lines to pay for the food.

The new computerized supermarkets are solving these problems. The key is the Universal Product Code (UPC).

The UPC is the little rectangle of zebra lines of different thicknesses that appears on almost every item sold in supermarkets. The lines contain a coded message. Computers can read the message. It includes the name, manufacturer, size, and price of the item.

The shopper brings the purchase to the check-out counter of the computerized supermarket. The cashier slides each item over a small window set into the counter. A device called a "scanner" reads the UPC with a laser beam as it passes over the window.

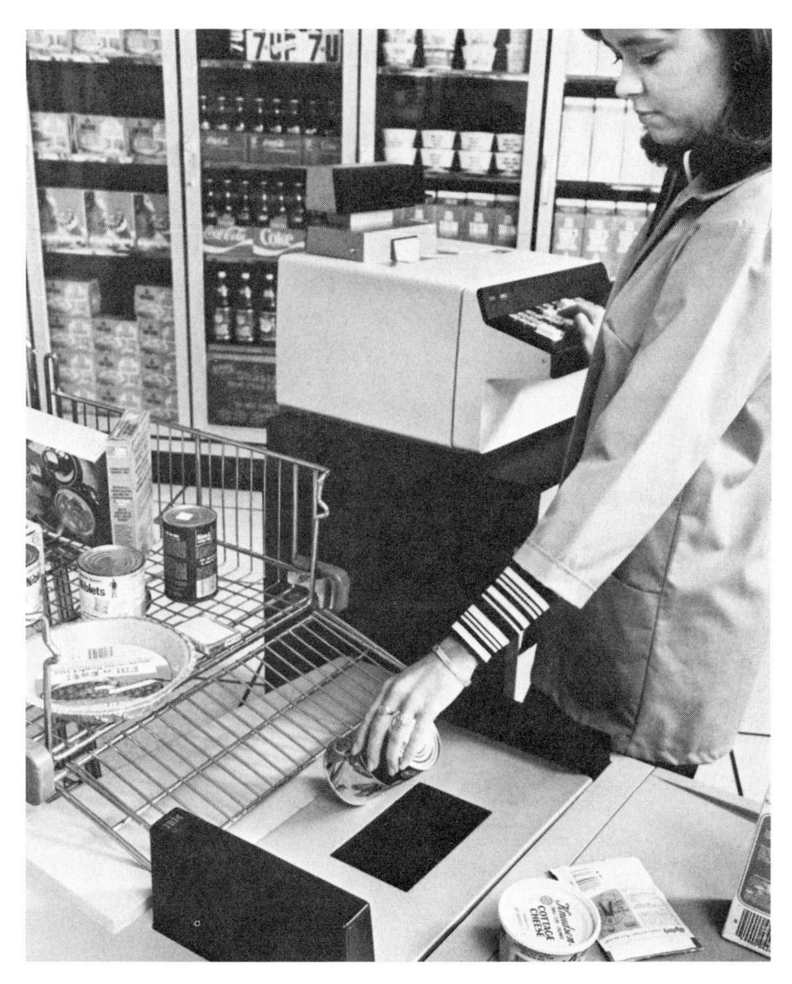

As the cashier slides a can over the scanner, information about the product goes into the computer.

The scanner is connected to the input of the computer. Automatically the product name and price appear on a screen for the shopper to see. At the same time, the computer prints a paper tape with that information, so that the person can check it later at home. Weighing vegetables, approving checks, deducting coupons or food stamps, and adding tax are also handled by the computer.

Giant Food Stores, a chain of over one hundred supermarkets, uses computers in its stores. The managers find it cuts waiting time by about 16 percent. Customers are served faster and better with even fewer cashiers.

But computers do not help only at the checkout counter. They can be very valuable in keeping track of the thousands of different items stocked by a typical store.

Each sale is entered in the computer's memory. At the end of the day, the manager can find out from the computer, for example, how many jars of peanut butter have been sold. These sales figures tell the manager whether to order more peanut butter, which brand sells best, whether an ad or a special offer raised the sales, whether there are more sales on certain days, and so on.

The UPC was first used around 1975. Yet only about 2,000 of the country's 30,000 supermarkets are now using the UPC system. Why?

One reason is the expense. It costs up to $20,000 to install a UPC system in one check-out counter. Another problem is that some consumer groups are against the change. With UPC there is no need to mark the price on each item. Therefore, the consumers say, it is hard to compare prices between different brands. Some labor unions are opposed to UPC. Stores with UPC systems hire fewer workers; thus there are fewer jobs for union members. And finally, many store owners and shoppers, in general, resist any change in the ways things are done.

Nevertheless, numbers of new stores are being built with scanners and computers installed; older stores are having them added. There seems little doubt that the UPC is here to stay.

## DEPARTMENT STORES

You bring a pair of socks to the sales desk in the department store. The cashier moves a wand over the price tag. The wand looks like a thick heavy pen attached by wires to the computerized register. It automatically reads the manufacturer, item, style, and price.

The information from the tag goes into the computer memory. At the same time, the price is flashed on a display panel. The computer calculates the amount due, including tax. It shows the change to be returned if you are paying cash. It runs a credit check if you are paying by credit card. The machine also prints out a receipt.

Once the information is in the central computer, it may be used to prepare reports on everything from the number of socks sold to the sales volume of the entire store. Managers, by pressing a button, can find out what items are selling fast at each register. They can find out how many remain in stock, the number sold in a given period, and where the demand is greatest. Then, they can decide whether or not to order more merchandise, whether to have a sale, or whether to drop a certain brand. The central computer can even tell them how well a cashier is working, and how many cashiers are needed at any time.

These computerized cash registers are known as point-of-sale (POS) systems. They can do amazing things. Owners of stores, from giant department stores to small shops, are putting POS systems to work for them. The systems are completely changing the way these stores do business.

The POS system prints price tags, prepares pay rolls, and speeds up billing. One department store was able to send out bills in two days, instead of three weeks, by using its POS system. The system also finds and corrects mistakes made in filling out sales slips.

One POS system use is less noticeable. Salespeople can use the system to signal the store detective if they spot a shoplifter. The message goes out to all the terminals, and alerts the nearest detective.

Retailers like the point-of-sale system because it helps them serve the customers faster and at lower cost. For customers, it means shorter lines at sales desks and fewer mistakes. And as more extra uses are built into POS systems, they should become even more widely used.

## RESTAURANTS

You can make reservations up to a year in advance at the Top of the Tower restaurant in Toronto, Canada. This popular restaurant, located one quarter of a mile above the ground in the Canadian National Tower, uses a computer to handle its many reservations. The same computer system also keeps track of food and supplies, does the bookkeeping, plans the menus, and prepares the payroll.

When you arrive at the Top of the Tower you first go to a lobby. Here there are three computer terminals. They show the reservations for each table over a six-hour period. They also show whether each table is free or being used at that moment. If your table is free, you are seated at once. If not, the computer seeks out the first table that will be free, and you are seated there.

Then, someone takes your order and gives it to the chef. At the same time, the code number for the dish you are having is entered into the computer. When you finish your meal, the computer prints out the bill that is given to you.

Wendy's is a chain of fast-food restaurants. About 100,000 people work at Wendy's 15,000 restaurants. They are located in 183 cities in 15 states.

With their computer system, Wendy's can tell the exact volume of business by the day, week, or month, in every store. The computer keeps track of all of Wendy's workers, full- and part-time. It figures out each worker's earnings, takes out deductions, and prepares their paychecks. It also keeps the records of summer workers who leave to go back to school, and then return the following summer. These workers can be rehired without filling out new forms.

The computer also reports on which stores have the

biggest sales. It spots trends and changes in eating habits. When the company gives away free coupons for drinks or other items, the computer can tell if the offer brought more people into the store.

Each year Wendy's opens a number of new restaurants. But first they check out the location for each one. A computer prepares a summary of the amount of traffic that passes the site. It lists any similar restaurants nearby. It analyzes the economic level of the area. The results help the owners decide whether or not to go ahead with their plans.

## BANKS

Bankers, like other business people, say that "time is money." And since they are in business to make money, they work hard to save time. That is why they are relying more and more on computers.

In many banks around the country, tellers sit at computer terminals. All the banking transactions go through the computer. This cuts the time and the number of errors that were normal in the past.

To speed things up further, banks are now installing computerized Automatic Teller Machines (ATMs) in bank lobbies, supermarkets, hotels, and shopping centers. These computers can perform many of the routine work of tellers. They provide bank customers with 24-hour banking service.

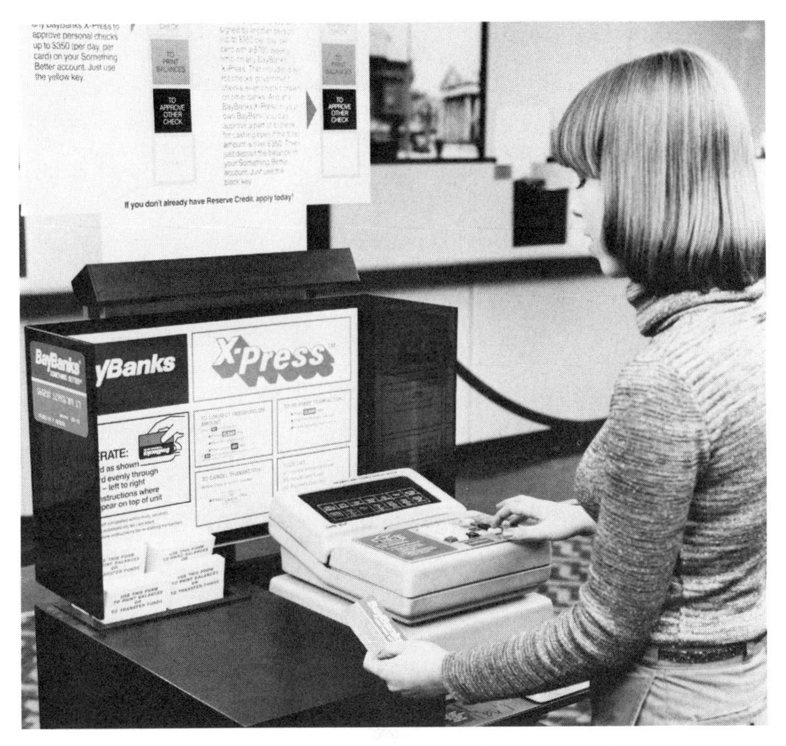


An Automatic Teller Machine takes care of simple banking needs.

To use the ATM, you need a plastic card issued by the bank. Your identification number is magnetically encoded on the card. Some banks also require you to select a password that you must key in each time you want to use an ATM.

In a typical ATM you slide your card through a slot in the machine. This lights up a panel which asks you to key in your password. If you don't know the password, you can't use the card.

Then, step by step, the panel directs you through the transaction. With the ATM you can deposit or withdraw money, find the balance in your account, get a check approved, or transfer money from one account to another.

Bank computers are also being used to transfer money from your bank account to a store's bank account. You can use the system, called Electronic Fund Transfer (EFT), when you shop in those stores whose computers are hooked up to your bank's computers. When you make a purchase, you do not pay with cash, check, or credit card. Instead you use your plastic bank card to transfer funds automatically.

Right now few stores use EFT. But many bankers and store owners believe it is a more convenient way to pay for purchases. They feel that it will grow rapidly in use in the future. In fact, they say that we are well on the way to a cashless, checkless society.

## FACTORIES

Many factory jobs range from dull to difficult to dangerous. There are metal plant workers, for example, who dip metal parts into powerful acid baths. Other factory workers spend their days removing red hot metal castings from furnaces. In auto factories, there are laborers who feed heavy steel plates into giant presses all day long. And other workers in the same factory stand amid flying sparks as they weld together the auto bodies.

Computerized robots are now taking over many of

A computerized robot dips metal parts into a hot acid bath.

these kinds of jobs. These robots often work faster than human factory workers, are inexpensive to operate, and have excellent safety records. They are freeing workers for jobs that require human skills and intelligence.

"Unimate" is a popular industrial robot. It is made of two parts: a powerful mechanical arm and hand that moves and bends in six different ways, and a built-in computer that stores over one thousand separate instructions.

Putting Unimate to work in the factory is easy. The user moves the robot through the various steps of the operation by pressing buttons on a "teach-control" device. Each touch of the button sends the arm or hand into another position.

Then, by pressing other buttons, the user locks the instructions for each step into the computer's memory. From then on, the robot goes through the steps of the program at top speed and without error.

Computers are also finding a place in the management of factories. The Factory Management System (FMS) of Honeywell uses computers to organize and manage the

A computer system records the time workers arrive at a factory.

various operations in a factory.

The new system automatically records the time that workers punch in to start their day. It later uses the information to prepare the payroll. On the factory floor, other computer terminals are fed data to follow work in progress, prepare production and worker schedules, and keep track of productivity.

The computer tells the manager how long each job will take, what materials are needed, and where to get them. In the warehouse, the computer is used to check the inventory of parts and materials and to organize the work in the shipping and receiving departments.

As more and more computers are used in business and industry, some workers are losing their jobs to the machines. A few years ago, a factory owner wanted to buy a computerized robot. The workers were against it. To win them over, the owner programmed the robot to serve coffee to the workers one morning. Everything was fine until the robot ran out of cups, but kept on pouring coffee! This made the workers realize that computerized robots might do some of the jobs in a factory. But most tasks would still need the skills and abilities of human workers.

# 7 HELPING AT SCHOOL

## ELEMENTARY SCHOOL

"Which is correct, 'He go out' or 'He goes out'?"

"He goes out."

"Right. 'He' is singular and 'goes' is the singular form of the verb 'to go.' "

"Which is correct, 'They go out' or 'They goes out'?"

"They goes out."

"No, that's not quite it. 'They' is plural, and the plural form of the verb is 'go.' Let's try these. Which is correct, 'The boys go to school' or 'The boys goes to school'?"

"The boys go to school."

"Very good, Carlo. 'Boys' is plural, therefore you need the plural form of the verb, which is 'go.' Now let's try this one. Which is correct, 'She run the race' or 'She runs the race'?"

This could be a conversation between a teacher and a student. Actually it is a conversation between a com-

Computer Aided Instruction is an important tool of modern education.

puter and a student. Under the general title of Computer Aided Instruction (CAI), computers have become important tools in education. They haven't replaced teachers as many feared they would. But they have improved education for many youngsters.

Typically, a student spends about ten minutes a day at a terminal with a keyboard and a display screen. The computer gives the student about thirty questions or exercises in that time. The computer then decides whether to move the student ahead, review an easier level, or provide more work on the same level.

The questions and exercises are divided into ten levels for the year. The computer always places students on the level that suits them best. It remembers where the youngster leaves off each day and starts from there the next day. Questions are mixed and varied, making it interesting to spend time at the computer.

## PEOPLE WITH DISABILITIES

Students with physical disabilities and handicaps used to be taught in special schools. Now most attend regular schools. Some are being helped by certain special computerized tools.

Sally was born blind. She learned to read braille, which is writing for the blind that uses raised dots instead of printed letters. But now she has a computerized tool for reading. It is called the Optacon (Optical to Tactile Converter).

The Optacon is basically a small TV camera. Sally moves it across a line of print with one hand. The camera is attached to a device that changes the images from the camera into a vibrating pattern. She feels the pattern with a finger of her other hand. For instance, she passes the camera over the letter *o*. Sally feels it with her fingertip as a vibrating circle of pulses. The Optacon lets her read any printed material. Nothing she reads has to be changed into braille.

Sally also has a computer device, called VersaBraille.

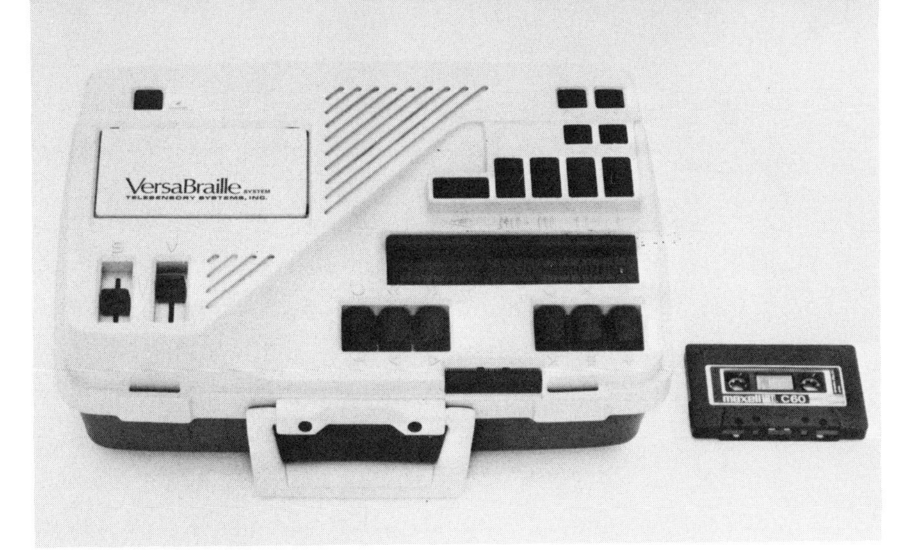


Students who are blind can use VersaBraille to take notes in class.

She takes notes in school with this tool. The keys on VersaBraille have the raised dots of the braille alphabet. Sally types in the information she wants to remember. It is recorded electronically on a cassette tape.

Later, to call back the information, Sally keys in her request. The VersaBraille quickly displays the material

Speech Plus is a calculator that announces every number that is keyed in and every result.

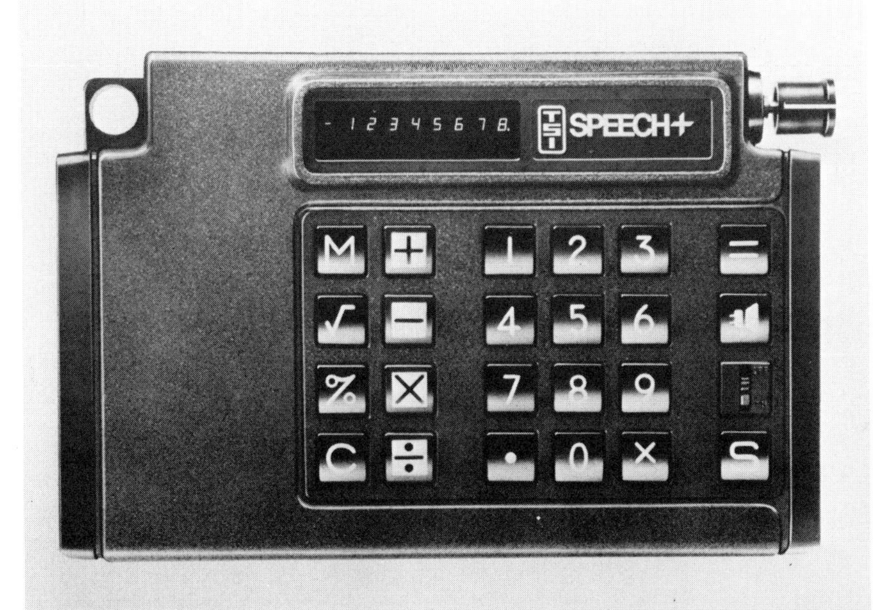

in lines of braille letters for her to read by touch.

People who are blind can solve math problems with the Speech Plus calculator. This computerized device does all the operations of an ordinary calculator. But it has some special features. The numbers and symbols on Speech Plus can be "read" by touch. It has a twenty-four-word speech vocabulary. Everything that is keyed in, as well as the results, is announced out loud. At school, students use this calculator in math, science, and business classes. At home, it helps people without sight to balance their bank statements, and to do other mathematical calculations.

Jeff has cerebral palsy. He has great difficulty in controlling the muscles of his body. The lack of muscular control makes it very hard for him to speak clearly. Jeff uses the computerized Autocom to communicate with others.

Jeff's Autocom fits into the laptray of his wheelchair. It is battery-operated, so it goes wherever Jeff goes. On its surface is a grid of ninety-one squares. Each square displays either a letter, a number, a word, or a complete sentence. Jeff slides a pointer over the Autocom. The writing in the square he chooses appears on a panel on the front of the tray. Here it is read by others.

An advanced model of this invention also has a sound synthesizer as part of the computer. It is able to speak the words, as well as show them on the panel. This is called a "talking wheelchair."

## HIGH SCHOOL

Plato is the name of an ancient Greek philosopher. It also is the acronym, or abbreviation, for Programmed Logic for Automatic Teaching Operations. PLATO is a computer system that is popular with the students in the Danville (Illinois) School District. It teaches them everything from French to how to fly an airplane. Students can discuss almost any subject with the computer. They find PLATO a very kind and very patient teacher.

When you sit down at a PLATO terminal, you have a wide choice of ways to use the machine. Teaching programs for over 150 subjects are in the memory of the computer.

PLATO also has a sound synthesizer to produce human speech. When you touch a button, the machine talks. For the language courses, it speaks perfect French, German, Russian, or Spanish.

Some PLATO terminals have special display screens. They are sensitive to touch. You answer questions on these terminals by pressing on the screen at certain points.

There are other display screens that have built-in photoelectric cells. You can "write" with a light pen—a sort of pocket flashlight—on these screens. The movements of the pen are sensed by the photoelectric cells.

Gifted students at Danville High School use PLATO terminals after school and during the summer. Members

Young Programmers Club members at Danville High School, Illinois, use computers after school and during the summer.

of the Young Programmers club spend from four to twelve hours a week with the computer. At first, they played games with the computer. Now they are writing their own programs.

"The types of programs we write vary from plotting sine waves to programming submarine war simulation," writes Lawrence Holloway, one of the Young Programmers. Learning to use computers is important for these students. But even more important is the vital lesson that computers teach—how to think logically.

## COLLEGE

Every college campus in the United States probably owns at least one computer. Colleges use them for everything from CAI, to training computer professionals, to record keeping.

One of the best known CAI courses is the one on logic given at Stanford University in Palo Alto, California. It is famous because it was among the first CAI courses, and because it is taught entirely by a computer. There is no professor, and there are no class meetings.

The course consists of 29 lessons. The students go through these lessons at their own rate. It takes each student anywhere from 30 to 140 hours of time at the computer to complete the course.

Stanford's logic course has a few special features. If the student keys in "hint," the computer provides a clue to help find the answer to a question. By typing "news," the student is told of any new developments or changes in connection with the course. If the student types "gripe," he or she can enter a complaint about the course.

A survey of students taking the logic course showed that they particularly liked to do the work at their own pace. Also, they found it convenient to be able to use the computer terminals twenty-four hours a day, six days a week. Although the Stanford students spent more time on this logic course than on most of their other courses, they gave it the highest possible course rating.

Adam is taking a course in music arranging at Dartmouth College in Hanover, New Hampshire. Every week he arranges a short piano piece for different instruments. Adam spends several hours each week at a computerized sound synthesizer.

The synthesizer is a device that produces all sorts of musical sounds electronically. By making various adjustments, Adam can produce any sound, from a single flute to a full symphony orchestra. He is able to hear the sound of his arrangements immediately. If he does not like the results, he can change the notes or instruments or rhythms. He can make as many changes as he likes until he is satisfied. Now, Adam no longer has to chase all over the campus to find players willing to try out his arrangements.

Jane is in her second year at a college in the Midwest. But she is still not sure what career she would enjoy after college. SIGI (System of Interactive Guidance and Information), at her school, is helping Jane and other students to pick their courses and plan their careers.

It took Jane nearly four hours at the SIGI terminal to answer all the questions the computer asked. What are your strengths? What are your weaknesses? What is important about you? Do you like to work outdoors or indoors?

After getting answers to a number of such questions, the computer screen showed a long list of possible career choices. The computer then asked more questions. The list of possible careers got shorter.

Next, the computer compared the requirements for each career with Jane's abilities and interests. It predicted how successful she would be in each possible career. More questions narrowed down the field even more. They also helped Jane to think more clearly about her future.

Toward the end of her time with SIGI, Jane was convinced that she should follow a career in law. The computer suggested what courses she should take to become a lawyer. It also drew up a list of both the rewards and drawbacks of a law career.

The Harvard University Business School in Cambridge, Massachusetts, recently got a letter from a bank with offices all over the world. They were looking for a graduate who spoke at least three languages, had some knowledge of banking, and was willing to travel.

In the past, such a request meant sifting through a long list of graduates to find those who fit the description. Now a computer program matches up employers and graduates in a matter of minutes. The computer even lists those graduates who have some, but not all, of the requirements for a particular job.

This program organizes all jobs in three ways. First it divides them into twenty-five basic industries: banking, manufacturing, medicine, insurance, food, construction, and so on. Then it forms groups of job types within each industry: sales, management, personnel, public relations, and so on. Finally, it breaks all the jobs down into fifteen geographical areas: Northeast, Pacific coast, Midwest, Europe, Mideast, and so on.

College students are aware of computers when they take a CAI course, or use a computer to decide on a career or find a job after graduation. But many do not stop to think that their names and grades and accounts are handled by computers—from the time they apply for admission through graduation.

# 8 PLAYING GAMES

## GAMES AND TOYS

Computers are changing the way we work, shop, study, travel, and communicate. What's more, they are changing what we do for fun. Just take a look at the great number of computerized games and toys in stores.

The first really popular computer toy, Simon, burst on the market in 1978. In Simon, four colored panels light up and different tones sound, one after the other. The order is set by the computer. You must try to remember the order, and press the panels in that same order.

If you do it correctly, you win. If not, Simon buzzes to show that you failed. This modern version of Follow the Leader can be set up to make the pattern harder or easier to remember. The same game, in different forms, can also be played by two or more people.

A microcomputer with a number of different programs is the basis of Alphie. Alphie is a robot toy. Pre-school age boys and girls try to beat Alphie in a number of

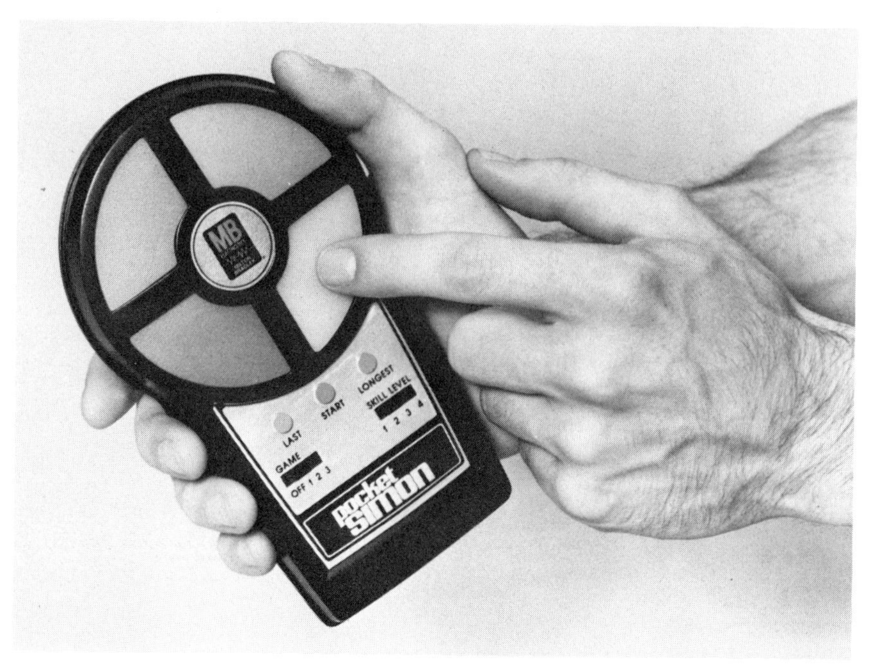


Simon, the first computerized toy, came on the market in 1975.

games. By changing the computer programs, the youngsters can play many different board games, question-and-answer games, and matching games with Alphie.

Big Trak is a tank-like toy with a remarkable computer memory. You can program it to go forward and backward and turn to either side, in any order. It has sixteen different sets of movements. You can send it for distances up to two hundred feet (61 m). Along the way it can change direction several times to avoid objects in its way.

Once it has reached its target, Big Trak is ready to attack. You can program it to fire its "laser" cannon. Flashes of light and bursts of sound add to the realism

A microcomputer hidden inside Alphie allows it to play a number of different games.

of Big Trak. After the toy destroys the target, its computer program can bring it back to its home base.

Part of the computer circuit of Speak and Spell is a sound synthesizer. It has a vocabulary of more than two hundred words stored in its memory. These are words that are often spelled wrong.

When you press the on button, Speak and Spell sounds four musical notes. They let you know that it is ready to play. Then, when you press the go button, the machine chooses a word from its memory. You hear a voice say, "Spell 'wash.' " The voice is produced by the sound synthesizer.

You spell the word by pressing letters on the keyboard. The machine says the name of each letter. It also displays the letter on a tiny screen. When you finish, you press the enter button. The machine might then say, "That is correct." You then are given another word. Or it might say, "Wrong, try again." If you do not get it right on the second try, the computer gives you the right spelling, spoken aloud. It then goes on to another word.

One computer game, Block Buster, is as popular with adults as it is with children. A wall made up of separate blocks is seen on a small 1½-inch-square screen. You control a paddle that hits balls against the wall. The object is to knock down the wall, block by block. As you go along, though, the computer makes the ball speed up, making it harder to score. Your score appears on the screen.

Block Buster is played on Microvision. Microvision can be used to play eight other games, including Baseball, Bowling, Sea Duel, and Mindbuster. You change games by inserting different tape cassettes into the Microvision frame, which changes the computer program.

About half of all microprocessor computer chips produced in this country are now being used by the toy industry. Toy makers say that they would buy more if more were available. They are turning out computerized games, toys, dolls, trains, planes, and cars. These products are great fun, and they are also introducing people to computers.

## CHESS

Many chess tournaments are held every year. But there have been some special new chess tournaments since 1970. These tournaments are for computers, not humans.

Twelve computers took part in the chess match held in Detroit in October 1979. The computers, eight from the United States, three from Canada, and one from the Netherlands, were connected by telephone lines to the tournament site. Each computer had its own terminal in Detroit.

A distant computer decided on a move. The move showed up at its terminal in words, such as Pawn to Queen's 4. A player then keyed the move into the other computer's terminal. This computer arrived at its move, which appeared on a terminal. Back and forth it went until one of the computers won.

To play computer chess, every square on the chess board is given a letter and a number, and each piece is given a number. Then a value is given to each position and each piece on the board.

There are usually about thirty-two possible moves at any moment. A good player thinks of the moves that he or she can make, and the possible moves the other player will make next. For the computer, this means thinking through 32 times 32, or 1,024 moves. Expert players try to think three moves ahead. A top computer chess program, therefore, must consider over a billion possible moves before making a decision.

A very large crowd in Detroit watched the match between the two favored programs, Chess 4.9, whose computer was in Minnesota, and Duchess, whose computer was in North Carolina. Chess 4.9 went into the tournament as the underdog because it was believed that its program was not as good as that of Duchess. But Chess 4.9 won its first three games. The final round was an exciting battle that finally ended in a draw. Chess 4.9, though, went on to win the trophy. Duchess tied for second place with Belle, a computer program at the Bell Telephone Labs in New Jersey.

David Slate *(right)* and Larry Atkin prepared the program for Chess 4.9.

A special event of the Detroit tournament was a game between Chess 4.9, and an international chess master, David Levy. The machine was assisted by its programmer, David Slate. According to the rating system of the United States Chess Federation, David Levy was favored to win. He had a slightly higher rating than either Chess 4.9 or David Slate. But it was hoped that together, Chess 4.9 and Slate would have a chance.

Slate changed the computer program so that he could suggest moves to the computer. The computer would test them out, and give its "opinion" on whether or not they were good moves.

It was a tight, good game. But finally on the fiftieth move, Levy beat the Chess 4.9–Slate team. Afterward Slate said that he probably paid too much attention to the computer's "opinions." Nevertheless, both men agreed that the computer played an outstanding game.

In May 1980, Carnegie-Mellon University in Pittsburgh, Pennsylvania, offered a $100,000 prize for the first computer program to defeat the world chess champion. Dr. Hans Berliner, of the university's computer science department, said he is sure that the prize will be claimed by the year 2000.

The computer programs for the tournament in Detroit were used with giant machines. But there are much smaller chess-playing computers. They are no bigger than an ordinary chess board. These computers, really microcomputers, are not expensive. They are widely used for fun and games.

The Sensory Voice Chess Challenger is one of the more advanced computerized chess games. The word *Sensory* refers to the fact that each square on the board contains a sensor. The sensor automatically notes each move you make. There is no need to key that information into the computer. The computer shows its moves by lighting up the square under the piece and the square to which it should be moved. Chess Challenger also has a fifty word vocabulary. It announces each move and each capture of a piece.

Chess Challenger can be programmed to play anyone from beginners to experts. Its circuits can analyze over three million different possible moves. The Chess Challenger can play quite a good game, although it is not as advanced as the tournament computer programs.

The Sensory Voice Chess Challenger is one of the more advanced computerized chess games.

A home computer system can include many separate parts.

## HOME COMPUTERS

It is exactly seven o'clock in the morning. Your bedroom curtains swing open. Your radio begins to play. You wake up and get out of bed. Although it is chilly out, the temperature in your room is just right. While you are choosing your clothes, the shower starts in the bathroom. As you leave the bedroom, the radio clicks off automatically.

You head to the kitchen for breakfast. The electric juicer has already squeezed an orange for fresh juice. The stove has heated the water for coffee, and the toaster has warmed the bread.

At 7:45 a buzzer sounds, telling you that it is time to leave. You place your dirty dishes in the dishwasher, where they are automatically washed and dried. After you put on your coat and leave, the heat and lights in the house go off, and with a loud click, the front door closes and locks.

Is this some dream house of the future? Not at all. Home computers that already exist can perform every one of those functions—and many more. They control the heating, cooling, and lighting of houses automatically.

One system uses sensors to find where people are spending time, and makes sure that that room is at a comfortable temperature and well-lit. Another home computer is hooked up to burglar and fire alarms. It alerts the residents and the authorities if either alarm is triggered.

A family in Los Angeles has a home computer system that lets them play up to three hundred video games. It helps with shopping suggestions, keeps financial records, fills out income tax forms, balances the checkbook, and files home recipes. It even computes how much food is needed for a dinner party.

In one computer expert's home, computers take the place of memo pads, notebooks, and even the kitchen bulletin board. He uses his home computer to hold lists of phone numbers and addresses, appointments, things to do, and anything else usually found in a desk calendar.

A home computer is teaching a couple in New York how to speak Greek. Learning programs on cassettes or disks are easily slipped into the computer. Other topics that they may study range from archeology to zoology.

There are more than 300,000 computers in home use already. The number is growing by about 100,000 a year. It will still be many years before computers are as popular as stereos. But they will surely be a source of fun and entertainment for millions by the end of the twentieth century.

# 9 FIGHTING CRIME

## POLICE EMERGENCY

"There's a man with a gun! He just shot a cop. He's crazy. Come fast."

The woman is very excited and breathless. The operator is taking the call on the police emergency number, 911. He tries to calm her down and get more information.

"Okay. We'll take care of it. Where is this happening, Ma'am?" he asks.

"In front of my house, 225 East 110th Street."

As she speaks, the operator keys the facts into the computer terminal. It is part of SPRINT (Special Police Radio Inquiry Network). This is the computer system used by the New York City Police Department to handle the thousands of emergency calls that they get every day.

SPRINT makes it possible to get police officers to a crime scene within minutes. And it gives the officers the

The New York City police use a computer system to rush officers to emergency situations.

information they need to do their jobs quickly and well, and in safety.

The operator keys in the numbers 10–13. These code numbers mean that a police officer needs help. It gets priority over all others.

The operator also keys in the location, the complaint, and all the details. The more information he can provide, the easier and safer it will be for the police officer who will be answering the call.

As the operator keys in the facts, they enter the computer. They also appear on the screen of the radio dispatcher. The computer has already added some information. It shows that the call came in at 11:32 P.M. The address is on the corner of 110th Street and Third Avenue. There are three patrol cars in the area. The nearest hospital is Metropolitan Hospital.

The radio dispatcher immediately calls all three patrol cars. She tells them it's a 10–13, and gives them all the details. Before she is even finished, the cars are speeding to the scene, sirens shrieking and lights flashing.

All the officers have their guns drawn as they come out of the cars. The gunman, seeing the police, drops his gun. The police place him under arrest, and take him off to the station house.

Meanwhile SPRINT is keeping track of the patrol cars on this case. The computer sets a time for the officers to finish the job, and report on it. If the computer does not hear from the officers within that time, it automatically sends out an overdue signal. The dispatcher then calls the units on the radio. If there is no answer, she may send other officers to check.

All calls received by the 911 operators are tape-recorded. They are also put on a special message repeater. This is useful when callers speak too fast to have the message typed into the SPRINT terminal. To get the missing facts, the operator simply turns on the message repeater. Conversations between radio dispatchers and patrol cars are also put on tape.

Sometimes, these recordings are used as evidence in court. Take a recent case of murder: a man called the 911 number and screamed that his neighbor was attacking him with a knife. By the time the police arrived, he had been stabbed to death.

The police arrested the next door neighbor. The District Attorney played the tape recording of the call in court. The tape, along with other evidence, convinced the jury that the neighbor was guilty of murder.

Suppose a person calls to report a crime. He knows that he is at the Hilton Hotel, but he does not know the address. The computer instantly provides the address from the list in its memory of large hotels, theaters, and public buildings.

Sometimes an older person will call 911, and give a street name that was used in the past, but has been changed. The person, for instance, may say "Sixth Avenue," instead of the new name, which is "Avenue of the Americas." The computer automatically changes the old name to the official new name of the street.

Only about one out of every five calls to 911 is to report a crime. Most are reports of fires, accidents, or sudden illness. In these situations, the operator pushes one of the buttons on a console next to the SPRINT terminal. This calls either the Fire Department or an ambulance for help.

Computer systems similar to SPRINT provide emergency police service in many cities around the country.

But they can all do more. The computer prepares summaries of all the calls it receives. It computes the numbers and types of calls, the time it takes to respond to and handle the situation, and the final results. It compares the calls by hours, by days, and by months. And it uses these figures to provide the best possible emergency service for the public.

## IDENTIFICATION

"There's a 10–50 at the Nite Owl Bar on Oak Street." The message crackles over the radio in the police car.

"That's us," says the police officer to his partner. They speed off to the address.

10–50 is the police signal for a disorderly person or group of people. The police get a 10–50 from the Nite Owl Bar a few times every week.

When the police arrive, they see two men wrestling in the street. The police quickly pull them apart. They ask both men for their names and addresses. One police officer takes the names and keys them into the computer terminal in the car. The other officer continues with the questioning.

The car computer is connected by radio to a computer in headquarters. This computer, in turn, is connected to the computers in the state police headquarters and in the NCIC (National Criminal Information Center) at the FBI headquarters in Washington, D.C. These computers are data banks. They contain lists and descriptions of wanted persons and of stolen property in each state and throughout the nation.

Within a few seconds information from headquarters appears on the car's computer screen. One of the men is wanted in Ohio for armed robbery and attempted murder.

The police search and handcuff both men. They take them to the station house for questioning. An expert takes a set of fingerprints from each man. He gives each print a computerized code number. The numbers are keyed into the computer terminal at the station house and go to the state and federal computers.

Within a few minutes a report comes back. It identifies the man wanted in Ohio. But it also shows that the other fellow has just escaped from a Florida prison. He was serving a twenty year sentence for assault and robbery.

What had started as a simple 10–50, ended with the capture of two dangerous criminals—thanks to the speed of the computer-based identification system.

## THE LAW

It is late at night at the Central Police Station in Fort Worth, Texas. Two police officers bring in a prisoner. They charge him with stealing a car and resisting arrest. The police officers fill out the complaint form. He is locked up in jail for the night.

The next day, copies of the complaint are sent to the District Attorney's (DA's) office. The DA studies the evidence. He decides to bring the case to court. He gives the complaint to a clerk. The clerk keys all the information into a computer terminal. The offense, the man's name and address, and all the details of the case are included.

Automatically, the computer system prepares the necessary legal papers. It also checks the name of the prisoner against the County arrest records. Has he been arrested before? On what charges? Was he found guilty and sentenced?

In this case, the computer finds that the man has a long record. He has been convicted and sentenced for a number of serious charges. The DA decides to charge him as a habitual criminal.

The DA's computer is also connected to a computer in the office of the court clerk. The complaint goes to the clerk's computer. The clerk uses the computer to find the first date when the judge, the DA, and the lawyers will be available for the trial. The computer also keeps track of the number of days the accused is in jail. The law says that everyone has a right to a speedy trial. If not, the prisoner must be set free.

Some judges keep a computer terminal on the bench. They use it to check the person's criminal record. This helps them in passing sentence.

When the jury brings in a guilty verdict on the pris-

Judges sometimes use computers in the courtroom to obtain information quickly.

oner, the judge reads about all his previous convictions. He decides to give him a long prison sentence to try to put an end to his criminal career.

Computers help put cases through court, and help the judge give fair sentences. Lawyers also use computers to let them guess the outcomes of cases *before* they take them to court.

A professor of law at Harvard University in Cambridge, Massachusetts, for instance, has programmed a computer with the outcomes of twelve hundred zoning cases in six different states. Zoning cases are those in which people ask special permission to build in places where it is against the existing zoning law.

The professor fed the computer 204 separate pieces

of information that played a part in the court's decision in the cases. These factors included the size of the land, closeness to the road, and whether the case was started by an individual or a real estate company. He then programmed the computer to make the same decision as the court.

Now, when someone wants to take a zoning case to court, the lawyer keys the facts into the input. The computer then makes a decision on the basis of the data and the program. The client can then decide whether or not to take the case to court.

At Michigan State University another law expert has prepared a similar program. It is used to try to arrive at the same decisions as the United States Supreme Court.

This lawyer programmed the computer on the basis of past decisions of each Supreme Court judge. As a test, he fed the computer thirty-four cases the court had already tried. The computer came to the same conclusion as the Supreme Court in thirty-three of the thirty-four cases. Its overall score was 97 percent correct!

From the police officer capturing a criminal, to the judge trying a case in court, the computer is proving to be a valuable tool of the criminal justice system.

# 10 RUNNING THE GOVERNMENT

## CENSUS

Every ten years the United States Bureau of the Census sets out to count all the men, women, and children in the country. It is a staggering task. Without high speed computers, it would take thousands of clerks more than ten years to collect the forms, tally the answers, and compute the results. With computers, much of the job is done in less than one year.

Numbers alone tell the whole story. On April 1, 1980, the Census Bureau received 120 million forms from Americans all over the country. The little circles filled in provided 3.3 billion answers to questions. By January 1, 1981, the forms had been read and counted by the Bureau's automatic and electronic equipment.

The census has to be accurate. Many important decisions are based on its results. It determines how many representatives will be sent to Congress from each state.

It decides how $50 billion per year in federal aid will be divided.

Many projects, such as airports, roads, and sewer lines, await the outcome of the census. Businesses also use census figures to help them decide whether to turn out more cribs for babies or more rocking chairs for older people.

As soon as a completed form arrives at the Census Bureau, it is sent to a high-speed microfilm unit. Automatically the form is fed into the machine. The pages are opened and flattened.

A camera takes a tiny microfilm photograph of each page of the form. The photographs of the forms fill about 5,000 miles (8,045 km) of microfilm. The original form is then shredded and dissolved in acid to protect the respondent's privacy.

The microfilm is next sent to a FOSDIC (Film Optical Sensory Device for Input to the Computer). As it passes through, all the information on film, except the name, is translated into an electronic language. It is stored on magnetic computer tape to be read later by a computer. Names do not enter the computer at all. They are only listed on the closely guarded microfilm, which is destroyed after seventy-two years.

The FOSDICs produce nearly 9,000 reels of magnetic tape. These are passed through the Bureau's giant computers. They count the people in every town, city, county, and state. They collect statistics on education and housing. For example, the figures in the 1980 census point

The microfilm unit at the Census Bureau opens each census form and snaps a picture.

The FOSDIC "reads" all the information, except your name, on the microfilm and enters it on a magnetic tape.

out that more people are living alone. The number of housing units is about 25 percent higher than it was in the previous census. Census figures also note a sharply reduced birth rate. The population figures show the smallest increase in American history, except for the 1930–1940 period of the Great Depression.

Until the 1990 census, almost every major planning decision of the government or private industry will be based on figures prepared by the electronic wizards of the Census Bureau.

FOSDICs used by the Census Bureau produce nearly 9,000 reels of magnetic tape.

## SPACE EFFORT

The success of the nation's space program has depended, from the start, on the use of giant, high-speed, advanced computers at ground control headquarters. These computers direct and control every aspect of blast-off, flight, and re-entry.

NASA (National Aeronautical and Space Administration) is also placing computers in the various space craft. It is now developing a special computer called STAR (Self-testing and Repairing). STAR will be placed in unmanned space trips lasting long periods of time.

STAR is programmed to locate and correct any fault in its own operation. It is hoped that the computer will be completely reliable, no matter how long the trip or how difficult the conditions.

NASA is also putting a small, eleven-pound (5 kg) computer on board the new Space Lab in which scientists will do experiments while in orbit around earth. This microcomputer will monitor an experiment on how the absence of gravity affects the growth of plant seedlings.

Various electronic devices will measure the light, temperature, and moisture in the spacecraft. A video camera will watch the plant growth. It will see if the seedlings follow their usual spiral pattern of growth. The measurements and images will be run through the computer. Then they will be changed to radio signals, and sent back to scientists on earth.

The government's use of computers both on the ground and in the space craft will allow us to advance still further in our exploration of outer space.

## NUCLEAR ACCIDENT

Nuclear alert! The word flashes out from the nuclear power plant at Three Mile Island near Harrisburg, Pennsylvania, in March 1979. A near panic occurs in the areas around the plant. Is there a danger of nuclear explosion? Is deadly radiation being released into the air? Should people flee their homes?

At the same time, the engineers at the plant are trying to learn what happened inside the nuclear reactor, and what steps they should take. Some gas is leaking from the plant. Is it radioactive? Some gas is trapped inside the reactor building. Is there danger of an explosion? They believe that the fuel elements of the reactor are damaged. Can the fuel rods be saved?

The plant engineers turn to the scientists at the government's Brookhaven National Laboratory for help. These scientists are leading researchers in the field of nuclear accidents. They have programmed a computer with a list of all the possible things that could go wrong in a nuclear plant and all the possible outcomes. This program, called a simulation, is kept in the computer's memory.

Six experts at Brookhaven feed all the known facts on the Three Mile Island accident into the computer.

But since they do not have all the facts, they do several runs on the computer. Each one uses different figures, to cover all the possibilities.

Finally, the scientists get the computer results. The computer outlines what probably happened inside the reactor. The accident was caused by a breakdown in the plant's cooling system. The reactor had not been cooled for about five hours before the accident. The fuel elements, therefore, were most likely badly damaged, and cannot be saved.

Further study of the computer print-out shows that not enough radioactive gas was leaking out to endanger the area. There is also little chance that the gas inside the building will explode.

There is every evidence that this is a very serious and dangerous accident. However, on the strength of the information from the computer, the people living around the plant are told it is safe for them to remain at home. Engineers get the necessary information to start making repairs. And the scientists at Brookhaven continue working to make their computer simulation program even more helpful in handling nuclear emergencies.

## SERVING THE COUNTRY

The federal government owns or leases about 16,000 computers. It is believed to be the biggest user of computers anywhere in the world.

Inside the high-security section of the Pentagon, top

generals and admirals meet once every three months to "play" war games. They use the latest computerized equipment to simulate events that might threaten the safety of this country. Then they use the computer to find ways to protect the United States. From these exercises come suggestions and policies for the defense of our nation.

The President of the United States depends on Wimex, a complex system of thirty-five computers located at twenty-seven sites around the world. Wimex collects and organizes warnings of enemy attacks or other crises, such as the seizure of an American embassy.

The system also provides up-to-date information on the location of United States forces. It holds in its memory a number of possible steps the United States might take in various emergencies. Once the President decides on a course of action, the system sends orders to move personnel, weapons, supplies, and aircraft to the trouble spot as fast as possible.

Nearly 5,000 different objects are in orbit in the space around the earth. The Unites States Air Force's North American Air Defense Command (NORAD) keeps a close watch on all of them. As the number of satellites increases, it becomes a more and more difficult job. Yet it is important for the protection of our country to know what is up there, who put it there, and whether it might be a threat to our security.

In the early 1980s, NORAD started building a world-wide network of computerized tracking stations. In each one a telescope magnifies an image of part of the sky, and changes the flickers of light into electronic signals, which are then fed to a computer. The computer compares a number of images of the same part of the sky. By seeing the change from image to image, the computer can distinguish between stars and man-made objects.

Other computers at NORAD headquarters, deep inside Cheyenne Mountain in Colorado Springs, Colorado, then determine the size, location, and purpose of any suspicious object. The computer system is so advanced that it is able to spot something the size of a soccer ball and identify it 25,000 miles (40,000 km) away!

The computers deep inside Cheyenne Mountain in Colorado keep track of any suspicious objects over the United States.

The Internal Revenue Service (IRS) has computerized its way of collecting taxes and checking returns. The new method means that taxpayers get refunds much faster. Not long ago the IRS installed a computer system for checking taxpayer identification information. This one computer allowed the IRS to cut its staff by two hundred people, which saved the government over $2 million.

Computers are also important to senators and representatives in Congress. Various computer systems help them to locate information on legal matters. A system known as LEGIS tells the status of all bills introduced into Congress. SOPAD gives the Senate and House members up-to-the-minute summaries of debates. JURIS includes digests of various legal documents.

Say you send a letter to your representative. A typical congressman receives 1,500 letters per week. It is very difficult to answer each letter personally. Computers help people in Congress keep up with their correspondence.

A staff member reads your letter. He or she composes an answer, using prepared paragraphs that are in the computer's memory. The letter is typed electronically by the printer terminal of the computer. Freed from writing and typing hundreds of similar letters, the staffers can spend more time on other matters.

In government, as in many other areas, computers are improving and speeding service and cutting costs. True, they do break down. They can sometimes cause more problems than they solve. And true, they can sometimes make you feel more like a number than a human being. It is very frustrating at times to have to deal with a machine instead of another human being. But, with all their faults, computers are helping to make our lives easier and better.

We are living at the dawn of the age of computers. Many of the greatest advances in computer science are yet to come. Computers will surely play an ever-growing role in all of our lives. It is up to all of us to make sure that we understand these remarkable machines.

# *For Further Reading*


## INTRODUCTORY BOOKS

Berger, Melvin. *Computers.* New York: Coward, McCann, 1972.

O'Brien, Linda. *Computers.* New York: Watts, 1978.

## MORE ADVANCED BOOKS

Adams, C. K. A. *Beginner's Guide to Computers and Microprocessors.* Blue Ridge Summit, Pa.: Tab, 1978.

Eames, Charles and Ray. *A Computer Perspective.* Cambridge, Mass.: Harvard, 1973.

Greenblatt, Stanley. *Understanding Computers Through Common Sense.* New York: Cornerstone, 1979.

Holoien, Martin O. *Computers and their Societal Impact.* New York: Wiley, 1977.

Spencer, Donald D. *Computers in Action.* Rochelle Park, N.J.: Hayden, 1978.

## TECHNICAL MAGAZINES THAT REPORT THE LATEST COMPUTER DEVELOPMENTS

*Byte*

*Computer Digest*

*Datamation*

*Infosystems*

# *Index*

MELVIN BERGER is the author of over sixty books for young readers, several of which have been named Outstanding Science Trade Books for Children by the National Science Teachers Association and the Children's Book Council.

A former teacher, Mr. Berger now devotes full time to his writing. He lives in Great Neck, New York, with his wife and two daughters.